MOSCOW! MOSCOW!

Christopher Hope was born in Johannesburg and grew up in Pretoria. He was educated at the Universities of Witwatersrand and Natal. His first book of poems was *Cape Drives* (1974), which received the Cholmondeley Award, and his first novel, *A Separate Development* (1980), won the David Higham Prize for Fiction in 1981. His long poem *Englishmen* was dramatised by the BBC in 1986. His next novel, *Kruger's Alp*, won the Whitbread Prize for Fiction in 1985, and the *Hottentot Room* was published the following year. *Black Swan*, a novella, followed in 1987, and in 1988 he published his first work of non-fiction, *White Boy Running*, which won the CNA Award in 1989. *My Chocolate Redeemer* was published in 1989. *Learning to Fly* (1990) under its original title *Private Parts and Other Tales*, was given the International P.E.N. Silver Pen Award in 1982. Christopher Hope has lived in London since 1975.

CHRISTOPHER HOPE

Moscow! Moscow!

Minerva

A Minerva Paperback

MOSCOW! MOSCOW!

First published in Great Britain 1990
by William Heinemann Ltd
This Minerva edition published 1990
Reprinted 1990
by Mandarin Paperbacks
Michelin House, 81 Fulham Road, London SW3 6RB

Minerva is an imprint of the Octopus Publishing Group

The epigraph on p. vii by Alexander Blok
comes from his *Selected Poems* translated by Alex Miller
and published by Progress Publishers, Moscow (1981).

The quotation on p. 7 comes from *Galina*
by Galina Pavolona Vishnevskaya (1985) published
by Hodder & Stoughton Ltd and reprinted by permission.

The quotation on p. 20 comes from 'Refugee Blues'
in *Collected Poems* (1976) by W. H. Auden
and is reprinted by permission of Faber & Faber Ltd.

The quotation on p. 43 comes from
'The Waste Land' published in *Collected Poems 1909–1962* (1963)
by T. S. Eliot and is reprinted by permission of Faber & Faber Ltd.

A CIP catalogue record for this book
is available from the British Library
ISBN 0 7493 9100 6

Printed in Great Britain
by Cox and Wyman Ltd, Reading, Berks.

For Nina, Katya and Volodya

Dear overseas guests, go to sleep,
may your dreams be blissful.
Forget that darkness falls
on the cage we struggle in . . .

Alexander Blok

Since everything will have been settled and paid for in advance,
it might be supposed that everything should go smoothly.
In practice that is not necessarily so.

Baedeker's Moscow

Introduction

I went to Moscow the first time quite by chance, and felt strangely at ease. Surprise was accompanied by a feeling of great relief; after fifteen years out of Africa, I had found a foreign city which reminded me of home.

It was, I suppose, the quality of the lies that attracted me, lies so lush, so many, sprouting overnight among the mossy, rooted feet of official spokesmen. There are lies for local consumption about food, and TV sets; and there is the travelling lie, the lie that says material transformation is taking place in the Soviet Union, that foreign policy successes make people happy, that President Gorbachev's reforms rival those of Peter the Great.

I returned to Moscow on a series of visits, summer, autumn, winter, without any of the proper and respectable intentions of touring, or exploring, or learning the complexities of Soviet politics, or studying the language, or seeing the sights, or listening to people telling me about the momentous changes now taking place in the country, or doing any of the useful things in the name of which such travels are often justified. I went back again and again, simply for the pleasure of knowing where I was without understanding why.

It was all very strange and yet wonderfully familiar. It read like a book I seemed to remember by someone whose work I had known since earliest childhood, not this particular volume perhaps but something from the hand of the same author. The feeling I experienced most strongly in Moscow was not love, anger, excitement – though I felt all these from time to time; my major and sustaining emotion was one of relief, of perverse consolation. I was reminded of the place I knew best, South Africa. The resemblance was shadowy and in many ways incorrect, yet there were reminders and recognitions so instructive, so comforting and terrible, that I fell into an hypnotic state of resigned relaxation, almost of enjoyment, rather like a sleepy child who fears he will be woken by nightmares but in a curious way welcomes them because he knows them, they are *his* bad dreams, his very own familiar horrors. I knew that at last I had found a place where the rich fatuities, gruff insincerities, grotesquely lovely phobias of a small, cosseted, supreme ruling class could be observed, noted and relished without permission and without anyone taking much notice. That this class was in the process of 'reforming' itself from within, just as the white ruling class from which I came in South Africa was in the process of doing, seemed an unexpected bonus. There were even in the Soviet Union 'homelands', governed from Moscow but called sovereign republics. That the mass of the people over whom this ruling class held sway preferred, if at all possible, that the rulers should not reform themselves but retire and vanish, and said so pungently and often, was a further familiar note in a political symphony which was my kind of music. Moscow was a city of gifts, it offered its admirers the option of expiring from grief or going chuckling to the grave. The only thing it withheld was the ability to tell the difference.

People abroad look at their televisions and say – oh! there are elections and street meetings and travelling intellectuals and press conferences, and talk of peace and the common European house, and it is all truly wonderful. The taste for such stuff among people abroad is as keen as ever it was when Stalin was a great reformer. It is said that a list circulates in Moscow among some who have sought to remember the names, not of Stalin's millions of victims, or his torturers, but of his foreign friends, from Shaw to Aragon, who welcomed the radical restructuring of his revolution. Nowhere, since I left South Africa, had I found a society where the talk was all of reform, of change, nor any place where less of it was to be seen.

Introduction

'Restructuring' is the word most used, *perestroika*, and it is called a legal revolution. The tablets of the new law have been handed down from on high and set in newsprint. It is without doubt a desirable thing; only I never set eyes on it. 'What', asks Viktoria, a librarian, dark-haired and indomitable, 'is there to restructure?' I looked and could not find it, except in the conversation of intellectuals. The new freedom is to be found in talk, words: they are *freer*, without being absolutely free, since even in conversations there are still-closed areas – Lenin, for instance, and Trotsky. But elsewhere what I found was a society steadily falling apart: run your fingers over it and you'd feel the widening stitches. In the night they snapped one by one.

In the meantime someone, somewhere, is trying to spin straw into gold. And we will know it has succeeded when those who tell us it is happening, tell us it has succeeded. At no point will those who tell us it is happening decently consult with those to whom it is supposed to be happening. 'That is not the Russian way,' Ivan the hunchback explained to me. 'Mark you, I said the "Russian" way, I didn't say the "Soviet" way.' He thought for a moment, and added, 'Not that there is any difference between the Russian and the Soviet way, but somehow I always like to make the distinction.' And Nadia, a translator, on discovering that I was from South Africa, asked, 'And how do you feel in Moscow?' The method of Muscovite interrogation often consists of unanswerable questions, but still, I answered, 'Everything seems familiar. The people in charge are forever talking of "change", but I don't see any signs of it.'

'We do have some change,' Nadia said, her green eyes wide and innocent (a sure sign, I was to discover, of subversive intentions). 'We have an elected Congress of Deputies now, but maybe eighty per cent are members of the Party.'

When I asked a government spokeswoman how this came to be possible in a free election, she said simply, 'It shows the trust of the people in the Party.' When I repeated this to Nadia, she laughed.

'Are you saying you feel at home here?' she asked. 'How strange for an Englishman.'

'I come from South Africa.'

'Welcome to Moscow,' she said.

Perestroika, restructuring, seems to be not a revolution, not even a reformation, but a reaction. 'What is to be done?' Lenin famously enquired. Today the answer comes back short and sharp: 'Plenty, and fast!' Because the place is falling apart. 'We pretend to work and they pretend to pay us,' goes the workers' joke – and jokes are no joke. The economy is in ruins, the provinces of the empire are opting out – and each time I return to Moscow the queues are longer.

'Dreams!' says Andrei the novelist with immense scorn. 'Today we dream of making paradise. Once we had hell, and we knew it. Wasn't that enough? Now we must build paradise. But I fear this paradise. What I want is not paradise. Why can't we have an ordinary life, like people in other places? No big changes, no big deals. At least we had got used to hell. At least it was our own.'

Chickens and muezzin and a slight shadowing around the eyes of some of my informants, like bruises or sleepless grief – these are the images I dream of when I dream of Moscow. The chickens were dead, the muezzin decamped, and the bruising metaphorical, but they are all there – in so far as anything can be *there* in Moscow.

But that came later. What came later did not throw light on what came before. It is natural to expect a linear progress, experience deepening into knowledge. But I never found this. For me there was Moscow, and again, Moscow. Material prosperity, scientific progress, modernity and mechanical progress were once supposed to be the distinguishing marks of the new world the Bolsheviks would build. In Moscow little of this is evident. Instead there are minds and sensibilities, some so finely wrought, so tempered that they may bend but they do not break under the assault of the few who control everything. New days, it is said, are coming with glasnost and perestroika. People abroad seem sure that they are already here. In Moscow they are not to be seen. That something of the greatest importance is unfolding in the Soviet Union cannot be denied. But the reasons and explanations offered for it are implausible.

Introduction

Better to take or make pictures, sketches of Muscovites; which I did when I thought they were not looking. I knew that later some would protest, 'But I don't look like that!' Or worse, others will say, 'That's me – to the life!' Both reactions will be wrong. I made these pictures so that I could believe what I saw and heard. They are, if you like, aids to faith. I take as true the advice of the poet Tyutchev who warned one hundred and twenty years ago that it was not possible to make sense of Russia, it was not amenable to reason, it was a place in which you had to believe.

At the time of writing (1988 – 89) the official Soviet exchange rate for the Russian rouble was 1 rouble to 1 pound sterling. The black market rate varied from 5 to 7 roubles to 1 pound sterling.

1
Very Like a Whale

It seems appropriate that I flew into Moscow's Sheremetyevo International Airport at night. The airport contains within it all the elements which make the city so naturally dramatic – or so effortlessly stagey – where every night is opening night on the dark side of the moon. The roof of the air terminal appeared to have been constructed of flowerpots, thousands of brown plastic tubs with, here and there, like a lonely bloom, a weak little light giving to the place a submarine illumination which added to its atmosphere of gloomy theatricality. Pushkin once declared that above the gates of Moscow there should be inscribed the warning: *Abandon intelligence all ye who enter herein.* But it is not intelligence that you lose, rather it is your sense of reality. You step into a drama to play a part for which you have not auditioned and if you take refuge in the audience you will find it composed of extras. In her memoirs, Galina Vishnevskaya has caught this feeling perfectly: 'We are actors by compulsion not by calling, in amateur theatre run by no one. And all our lives we perform our endless, pathetic comedy. There are no spectators, only participants. Nor is there a script, only improvisation. And knowing neither plot nor denouement, we act.'

The passport officer will scrutinise you for long moments; an intent yet disconcertingly blind gaze, he seems to be looking through you – and indeed, as I later discovered, in a way he was, reading off my height against a chart incised on the glass of his booth and checking it against the information given on my visa.

Sheremetyevo purported to be an airport like any other the world over, yet everything – the overhead garden of illuminated flower-pots, the tourists waiting to play their parts, the uniformed officials too young for their large caps, their seemingly borrowed uniforms – all contrived to deny it. Overworked, secretive, unsure, the officials dig their chins into their chests and only occasionally let slip a direct glance. I never got used to it – that is not something Moscow allows. Yet somehow an aura of friendliness escaped from these curiously self-absorbed officers. How does suspicion breed friendliness? Eventually an answer came to me, courtesy of the country from which I came: everyone was suspected, it was not personal, merely customary.

Riding the escalator up to ground-floor level to find the car which was to drive me into Moscow, I saw my first floor lady. Motionless in a green wooden chair at the top of the escalator, she watched the incoming travellers ascend in their hundreds each day. She wore china-blue knitted woollen stockings, ribbed, rising over her ankles and heading for the hills of her knees; her hands were folded quietly in her lap, her grey hair was scraped back and her eyes were unexpectedly young. In that placid face it must have been the non-stop ocular exercise that kept her eyes so youthful. She meant no harm; like everyone else she had her place, she was just doing her job. So many thousands of jobs, so many people to watch, so many eyes, so many knees, so many knitted woollen stockings. How curious that in the capital of the USSR, seventy years after the most profound revolution the world has witnessed, unleashed in the cause of human freedom, everyone knows his place. For the traveller newly arrived in Moscow, the greatest shock is the discovery of how oppressively secure things are; people seem settled to the point of immobility. Who can blame them? The Revolution was fought to make Russia safe for the floor ladies (of both sexes). After a reign so long established, after a lifetime so comfortably seated, why should anyone give up his place? Besides, movement of any kind, particularly political movement, was for a long time very dangerous and during Stalin's long rule positively fatal. It is no longer dangerous but it is uncomfortable, so it is not surprising that those who cry out for progress encounter resistance. The heirs of the Revolution are the sedentary classes. The beneficiaries of perestroika are the chattering classes.

The girl at the Intourist desk at Moscow airport wore a magenta silk blouse, apricot culottes and burnished steel lipstick. Her outfit was dated but it was recognisably modern, 'Western', taking up its desirable colour-scheme and contour from continual exposure to foreign tourists. She was superior and she was seated – the two things go together, indeed they are often indistinguishable. Occasionally she would stand on tiptoe and peer at us as if an invisible wall divided her from the foreigners. Over her shoulder I glimpsed a back room packed with men at a table, yawning, stretching, smoking. Around the smooth corners of the counter were more men, dressed in a motley collection of fur, leather, woollen coats and hats, all with hungry eyes and anxious moustaches, all looking to the girl for guidance and deliverance, all contributing to a scene of restrained pandemonium. The foreign tourists must call at the Intourist desk for their cars, and the girl will then summon the drivers.

'Kirill!' she cried, imperious, impatient, without looking up from the list of names she held and against which she checked our vouchers.

Kirill did not come and the hungry-eyed men pressed closer, while those in the back room leaned over and cocked an ear. They looked like poker players or off-duty taxi drivers, or sentries expecting the call to duty. And still no Kirill, but it did not matter because in his place came Misha or Lev or Volodya. The aspirant drivers' pool was a hatchery of threshing, jostling creatures. One would be netted by the intrepid fisher girl and tossed into the lap of the bemused foreigner.

The driver she caught for me was called Vasily. 'I speak little English,' he told me in courteous, apologetic, unaccented English, and then declaimed in a musical baritone, 'They bore him barefaced on the bier, hey non nonny, nonny, hey nonny.'

'Shakespeare,' I said helpfully.

'*Hamlet*,' Vasily corrected me gently. He tapped the cassette player in the dashboard and added, in Russian, 'This is my school. I am learning English from tapes. It is difficult.'

He kept the car in the fast, official lane, flicking his lights at drivers who were slow to give way ahead of us. The big square apartment blocks along the airport road sped past. People lived in them, I knew that from the bright lights branching from the ceilings behind each window, standard fixtures in standard blocks. Only the differently coloured curtains in the windows told you that the occupants were not standard; they had taken over once the builders had gone away, and put their different marks on their homes. Up on the roof of one building a small gaudy neon hinted at some unexpectedly rakish commodity imported from Bulgaria.

In Moscow most people are indoors soon after dark. At first I imagined that this had something to do with the politics of the place but, in fact, ever since the early eighteenth century, travellers have been remarking with some wonder upon the emptiness of Moscow after dark. Both in the desolate outlying suburban estates and even closer to the centre, you will face what someone once called 'the stillness which reigns after ten o'clock'. In the eighteenth century the place was livened up a little by the whores who hung around Smith's Bridge where the French milliners had their quarter, but that little world has gone the way of the milliner and the ostrich feather. Yet the darkness is deceptive. There is lots to be found in the dark, if you are prepared to get lost in it.

Vasily delivered me to my hotel in the centre of Moscow. I wished him good night.

'Good night – *sweet* ladies,' Vasily added firmly.

'Good night, sweet ladies.'

'You're welcome,' said Vasily.

Moscow hotels, large or small, purloin the name, for they are really detention centres for tourists. Few will ever forget that first encounter with one of these uniquely awful establishments; memories remain rather as they do of early and unhappy love affairs, where subsequent experiences only confirm the bitter-sweet consternation of the first.

I was decanted by Vasily the Shakespearean into the hotel of the singing muezzin. I never think of it without a certain bleak affection. For a start I had trouble getting past the army of green-jacketed doormen who guarded the entrance. At first I thought they were an obstacle special to my hotel but that was wrong: in fact they are to be found in the foyers of all hotels. Later I imagined that their function was to make things difficult for hotel guests – a sharp reminder to decadent tourists that life was not a bowl of cherries; that not only were there no cherries, there was no bowl either. This was closer to the truth than my earlier supposition. But eventually I realised that their true purpose was to hold back the armies of uninvited people bent on invading the hotel which is seen as a centre of foreign luxury, hard currency, camaraderie, congeniality, investment potential, warmth, light, booze and excitement, all of which simply do not exist in the rest of the city.

These invaders inhabit the big hotels as if they were termite hills with hidden corridors and passages. In fact there *are* hidden corridors and passages, because all the official entrances (most of which are actually opened on the whim of the doormen to allow a stream of entrants from either the left-hand door or the right-hand door) have shadow entrances and exits – around the side, at the rear, through the roof quite possibly, or beneath the cellars – so there is a continual coming and going, a merging of the legal, the semi-legal, the tourist, the friends of the tourist, interpreters and police.

Taxi drivers form the swirling outer ring of suspicious characters. Next there are young men with sharp haircuts and camel-hair coats who have ways of getting around the doormen and preen themselves in the lobbies; they may run the girls who prey on the tourists, exchange black market currency, play the fruit machines, or, for all I know just sit around pretending to be tourists themselves. And then the girls: these may be divided into visiting prostitutes, tourist groupies and 'staff'. (All Moscow hotels are heavily staffed, but personnel are not there to serve the guests, the idea of service being as yet unknown.) These transients constitute a world apart. The bigger the hotel the richer the lobby life and, in the end, it becomes impossible to distinguish between guests and visitors, real or fake employees, except for those in uniform, and even they, when the need arises, exchange their uniforms for an hour or so with friends and relatives, or paying strangers.

Finally, there are the paid staff like the Intourist girls, who during the day staff the desks, telex machines and flower stalls; the waiters and the waiters' friends, cousins and brothers and aunts and uncles, not to mention those whom you do not see, the kitchen staff, with *their* dependents and clients. What looks at first like a normal hotel soon dissolves into a shadow-play of profiteers, imposters, pimps, baffled tourists, whores and sight-seers, and the asylum seekers who find these pale simulcra of Western pleasure gardens to be irresistible.

Such was my first hotel, the place where I was to fall among the muezzin. In the bathroom the tiles were pink, flesh-coloured, the colour of English skins surprised by the African sun, and in the corners where the floor met the tiled wall of the bath the dust had been climbing, mounting like the sand in an hourglass. No mundane dirt, I realised with a faint chill, but human dust, the dust unto dust, flakes of skin of tourists past, of imperious foreigners, dead and turned to clay; and all their clothes, hamburgers, and suntans had come to this: 'about as little dust as might stop a hole to keep the wind away'.

A knock on the door came as a relief. It was my floor lady, little, dark, lithe, wearing a cherry headscarf, and with the bold but wary eyes of the footpad turned doorstep Bible-pusher.

'Good evening, would you like to sell something?'

'What do you have in mind?'

'Cigarettes, currency, clothes, batteries. Anything at all would be welcome.'

She might have been collecting for her local charity bazaar. But charity has gone the way of milliners in Moscow, vanished with the bears and dwarfs and buffoons that once delighted the Tsars. I was in the capital of the country which championed the non-acquisitive society, which ran upon a system devoted to the non-competitive allocation of goods and services according to need, not income, yet I was being solicited by a woman disguised as Red Riding Hood with the sort of eyes that would have scared the wolf out of his skin. These sharply educative shocks are part of the texture of Moscow and ensure, at least for me, that every time one returns it is for the first time, and nothing is ever the same again. But I was still naive enough to baulk at business and when I heard the word I reached for my charity. I handed her a carton of American cigarettes.

'How much?'

'No charge.'

'For nothing!'

Without warning she stood on her tiptoes and pressed her lips to my cheek. The kiss was given before I knew it and then, almost immediately, while still on her toes she quickly wiped the incriminating lipstick from my face. Then she was gone and I was left wondering if it had happened at all, except that I held in my hand a tourist brochure thick with colour photographs tinted with what seemed like fierce, unexpected vegetable dyes: lettuce lawns, yellow pepper palaces and radish churches. The brochure came straight to the point: *Welcome to Leningrad!* it said.

My small room contained an unnaturally large and completely empty fridge. This was in an hotel which housed a number of Soviet guests whom I knew to be important simply because they were there. Less eminent local travellers stayed in the distant suburbs at one of the bleaker hotels where fierce doormen let no one pass. The names of these places were alarming little jokes like The Dawn and The East. Siberian industrialists and Romanian shoe-salesmen were confined in such hotels, if they were lucky. If they were luckier still, they weren't. A Polish industrialist used to pay for his room and then go into hiding with friends for the duration of his visit. 'Luck' in Moscow is often a matter of class – that is why many people have little of it. Most people, when they travel to Moscow spend the night with relatives or friends, or sleeping upright in a plastic chair at the railway station.

Some time that evening, several floors below me, a Moslem cantor, a muezzin, or apprentice muezzin, began calling the faithful to prayer. It seemed the wrong time but I understood why he was singing: he needed the practice. Such was the construction of the hotel: raw concrete and minimal insulation, giving a remarkable resonance that brought the muezzin, in all but body, to my bedside.

Around midnight other voices began to reach me. They came from the ventilation shaft set into the wall above my bed. I realised that the shaft was connected directly to some room where hotel staff and tipsy guests gathered late at night, told stories, cracked nuts and smashed glass. The muezzin had the greater carrying power, his thin reedy song was remarkably penetrating. But the party-goers were more troubling and the full force of their revelry seemed to be directed by the connecting shaft into my room alone. It took me some time to find a way of masking the noise. In the end I switched on the fridge, an enormous arctic wonder moored in the middle of the room, a mechanical iceberg. It made the kind of sound that helped me to appreciate why the tank-capacity of the Warsaw Pact keeps Western military planners awake at night. But at least it had a consistent rhythm, it did not get drunk or smash glass and laugh at its own jokes. I used my fridge in a way that modern fighter planes use flares to divert the homing devices of hostile missiles, as a form of sonic interference. In the dead of night its polar rumble was strangely reassuring.

It might have gone on like this for ever. But the muezzin was ambitious, or just plain bad. Some nights later he got a whole lot of his friends into his room and they held a joint service, a kind of Moslem eisteddfod for up and coming clerics. They went on into the small hours. Someone had determined they would get it right, or go on until they dropped.

The hotel was full of out-of-town Party big-shots, Eastern Europeans many of them but, wherever they hailed from, they were still a long way west of the Moslem choral singers. From all over the hotel came angry cries: 'Go back to Tashkent!' and 'Silence, verminous Uzbeks!' Sleepless guests fought back with shoes and bottles, banging on the bare floors of their little rooms until the hotel, like the concrete prison it was, rang with the cries of the tormented. But the choir only sang more loudly and it was not until about four that the police arrived and shut down the show. I never knew what happened to the muezzin but, in a way, I missed him. For one thing he no longer sang me awake in the morning. I asked about him in the lobby. The girl at the desk put down her nail file and lifted her nose. 'The Moslem contingent have left Moscow.' What a chill those words brought with them. Where could one possibly leave Moscow *for* that would not be infinitely worse?

Neither luck nor judgement explain my enchantment with Moscow – it was more a kind of fatal compulsion. I had been in the city for just a few days when I went for a walk at about nine in the evening and discovered that everyone seemed to have gone home. Red Square was deserted, the guards outside Lenin's Mausoleum had frozen into watchful immobility, only their eyelashes moving under their peaked caps. The door to the Mausoleum which stands open during the day to admit the endless line of pilgrims was now closed tight, the tabernacle sealed for the night. The little red flower of the Revolution slept in his glass coffin.

Red Square was windswept, lonely, vacant. I knew it had not always been like that. When Lord Curzon visited the city in the 1850s he took photographs which showed Red Square crowded with pedestrians and lined with elegant streetlamps with graceful, curved necks like steel swans. Carriages dashed over the cobbles and a flower market bloomed beside the Kremlin wall. Today such open spaces are meant for tourists, troops and gun carriages, for parades and speeches and crowds. High above the yellow walls the stiff evening breeze, mixing with the spotlight, had a way of liquefying the national flag, making it ripple like hot red cream. I felt the ghosts of the place crying aloud, like Hamlet's father, for vengeance. Red Square has always been a place of execution. Through the centuries victims were routinely knouted, hanged, beheaded, racked, mutilated, flogged before gaping crowds. In the Kremlin wall lie buried the remains of Party luminaries ranging from Lenin's wife to Joseph Stalin, who until 1961 lay beside Lenin in Shchusev's sturdy mausoleum; murderers, heroes and victims bricked up together. Across the square the arcades of GUM, the vast State Universal Store, were empty. The windows displayed pyramids of rusks; their Saharan dryness seemed to reach through the plate glass window and made me thirsty.

I went back to my hotel and sat in the dining-room among people finishing late suppers. Muscovites do not dine without music if they can help it; at the far end of the enormous room was a jazz band, a couple of electric guitars with amplifiers, drums and a female singer in white boots and white pants and a pretty predictable line in polystyrene pop. At about ten-thirty the waiters downed tools, locked the doors of the restaurant and refused to serve any more food or drink. Then began the lengthy process of decanting the diners. New hotel guests still attuned to western time arrived at the locked doors and rattled them vainly. They were too late.

I was joined unexpectedly by three young people, two girls and a boy all in their twenties who introduced themselves as Galina, Olga and Alexander. They were out for some fun among what Muscovites call the 'evening public' – that comparatively small band who go dining after dark. Galina was the eldest, petite, training as a radiologist. Plump, shy Olga was learning to be a nurse, spoke English fairly well while Galina had a disconcerting habit of lapsing into French. Olga looked up to Galina as the leader and lady of fashion. Alexander was a crumpled, pleasant boy who spoke only two words of English, 'Killer bee', and he used them to express appreciation or exasperation. He was a student of science. When I asked what kind of science, Olga said, 'Music.' They didn't like the band, Galina explained, wrinkling her nose at the amplified music and scornful of the portly dancers pushing their way around the floor, most of whom, she explained, were locals. There was better music elsewhere, she said, and suggested that they show me something of 'Moscow by night'. They would show me the real thing.

'People talk of opening the doors and letting us travel freely to the West. But would you really want us? If I were you I wouldn't want *them*.' And she jerked a thumb at the dance floor.

Leaving was not easy – but then, as I was to discover, in Moscow it never was. Frantic tourists dashed themselves against the glass door like doomed moths. We tried the back door but that was bolted. With an impatient shake of the head, Galina led us out through the kitchens where what seemed like dozens of ladies stood in a long row behind cash registers which rang out in a dozen assorted trills and bells and percussive bangs of the cash drawer. Moscow needs artists for such scenes, it needs its own Degas to sketch such hidden beauties: *Till Ladies Cashing Up* and *After the Dinner*. Down corridors we went and round corners for what seemed like kilometres, until at last we came to a little door where an old man waited in the shadows with a key and, instead of refusing to allow us to pass, opened the little door and sent us on our way with a smile and a wave. We emerged on the far side of the hotel and I was immediately lost.

When I think now just how difficult it is to get lost in Moscow, of how many try and fail, I realise how lucky I was. It was an introduction, an initiation, into the mysteries of just what makes Moscow life so unexpected, so captivating. But at first all I saw that night as we emerged from the hotel were the problems that ranged ahead: the empty streets swept clear of buses and taxis, the river silent and empty. The Moskva River is deserted for much of the year, when no boats or fishermen, no flotsam, no ducks or swans, lovers or swimmers venture upon its black and silent waters. At night it is even more remote and slides by like a guilty secret. This is the face that Moscow presents to the foreigner, a face which, on the surface, suggests nothing but empty desolation, where everything is forbidden, unavailable or unknown. It is not surprising that most people succumb to this myth. Even by day it is difficult to get around Moscow above ground except in officially organised cars, buses or groups. The streets are wide, the drivers speed-crazy, and two out of three taxis will not stop, and those that do, despite bargaining, bribing or blustering, possess drivers who are guided by caprice or indifference and treat most destinations suggested with affected ignorance, or brisk contempt. But on that night with Galina, Olga and Alexander (who had had more champagne than was good for him and who sang without interruption the opening bars of Dave Brubeck's 'Take Five', slapping his knees to emphasise the beat) one of the great truths of Moscow life was revealed to me. Yes, on the surface everything is 'impossible' or 'out of the question' – the reason being 'the system' – but the instant that Galina stepped into the road and lifted her hand a few inches from her waist, several private cars appeared from nowhere and offered their services. A price was fixed and we swept into the night. Beneath the surface, it seemed, everything was negotiable.

In the coffee house, the 'coffee' was ersatz, slightly plasticky to the taste and very sweet but drinkable if well spiked with vodka or brandy. That's how you knew it was a 'real' place, said Olga: fake coffee. Real coffee was only for tourists. A battered cassette player, all chrome and black plastic giving it the right period feel, the audio equivalent of a 1950s fish-tailed Oldsmobile, stood on a table playing American blues. The lights were dim, the crowd was young, students and translators and teachers who sat around, danced or just hung out while Blind Lemon Jefferson sang 'Hangman's Blues' and Alexander gave me the thumbs up because this was 'the real thing'.

All the kids possessed one cherished item, a haircut, a brooch, a leather jacket, a pair of jeans or boots, a smattering of English. They wore this one treasure with a vengeance and made sure that a little went a long way. It had to: the absence of things that are pretty, shapely, decorative, trim, dainty or brightly coloured is a severe frustration and the consequent hunger for them, particularly among the young, is ravenous. One item is all you need to join the real world and if the State won't provide it then you can make it yourself. A gold earring, a scarf, a waistcoat, worn with such panache that the impression one takes away is not of deprivation but of raging stylishness.

Into the gaps left in your life by what you lack, or what is forbidden, conversation pours like a torrent. It was here I met Valentin, a linguist who became a friend, a profound exponent of that wonderful melancholy Hamletic humour in which Muscovites excel and who defined one of the great principles of Soviet life for me: 'Everything not expressly permitted is forbidden.' A young physics teacher named Dmitry talked of Hegel, of the lyric poet Alexander Blok who died soon after the Revolution, and of Fats Waller. His girlfriend, Lena, hoped to become a dancer; 'In the meantime I work in a library, but only in the meantime . . .' Was it true, Lena demanded, that the Queen of England could theoretically be deposed by an act of Parliament, and would she flee into exile? And if that happened would there be anything to stop the British prime minister from adopting her

[18]

role and powers? Then Olga talked at some length about Sikhs, confessing that she found their turbans to be wonderfully exotic. She fell silent in perplexed wonder when I told her that Sikhs did not cut their hair but wore it caught up in a fine net beneath their turbans. Dmitry said that he was looking forward very much to the imminent visit of the American President. There was something in Ronald Reagan's face that reminded him of the poet Blok. Did I think anyone had ever pointed this out to the President? Galina declared her detestation of all Russian men over thirty. They had forgotten how to smile. Perhaps they had never learnt, suggested Lena. Over in the corner Alexander was dancing by himself. Occasionally he would lift his cup to me in a silent toast and mouth the words, 'Killer bee!' Eventually he passed out and Galina decided that this was the signal to move on.

We ended up at a party of the black-leather crowd, heavy metal rockers who are present in ferrous outcrops upon the rockface of Moscow life away on the outskirts of the city. There was the usual leather-padded front door, the bright bough of unforgiving overhead lights branching from the ceiling and reproductions of icons brooding darkly on the walls. Unlike the coffee-bar kids down the road, this mob is expected to face the world completely equipped. Leather jackets, studded belts and Nazi insignia do not come cheap, even in the West; the outlay must be large and the difficulties of supply fearsome. The party was in an apartment on the second floor of a block about a twenty-minute ride from the centre of town, but the inhabitants were entirely and perfectly kitted out in the heaviest of heavy metal gear, clanking with swastikas and chains and toothy with zips. The effect of all this steel and leather tackle in the suburban apartment was bizarre, boys and girls in crackling black and glinting trim looking for all the world like motorbikes in a chapel. I never knew why we were there, perhaps we just went along to watch. The volume of the music and strong smell of pot told me that many people were beyond sprightly conversation. So we stared at them, they stared at us and it was all very friendly. Galina said, 'They like their drugs. Not just the smoking, either.' She made a syringe of her fingers.

'Do they share needles?'

Galina smiled sweetly. 'In the Soviet Union we share everything.'

'It is very modern, no?' Olga enquired anxiously, proud of the fact that not everyone in Moscow was over the hill.

'Yes, I'm afraid so. Very modern.'

About three in the morning we left the *heavy metalski* to their seance. At that hour the taxis had vanished and none of the private drivers still cruising the streets seemed willing to make the long run back to my hotel, and that was how I came to spend the night, or what remained of it, with Galina and Olga in their apartment on the very furthest edge of the city. Through my head, with that painful but disciplined rhythm you get with a pounding tension headache, went Auden's lines from *Refugee Blues*: 'Say this city has ten million souls,/ Some are living in mansions, some are living in holes.' Up a flight of stairs we went, with Galina apologising in advance for the disappointment she felt sure awaited me and reminding me again and again that they had very little.

The apartment was indeed small, even by Moscow standards; a bathroom out on the landing, a bedsitting room and a kitchen. In the bedroom was a cupboard, a divan bed and a single deckchair incongruously cheerful, its red-and-white striped canvas more suitable for the beach or the lakeside. There was a single easy chair at the little rickety table and the two girls seemed to live on a diet of biscuits and Western pop. A cassette player stood on the floor and there were a couple of shelves full of middle-ranking British and American rock groups. Olga insisted on cooking eggs. Then she cleared the kitchen and went to sleep on a mattress beneath the table. I think she was living illegally in the apartment but it was difficult to tell because the line between what is illicit and what is permitted is so fine as to be almost indiscernible to a foreigner. Eventually Galina made up her divan bed and I took the striped deckchair. She put on a tape, to soothe her, she explained, and to help her sleep. Perhaps I would be kind enough to explain the meaning of the words to her as she had trouble with the lyrics of several songs. Please, she said, 'What does it mean, "Pump up the volume"?' I looked at my watch, it was nearly four, hardly worth going to sleep anyway, and so for the next couple of hours I explained as best I could the bright insincerities of popular love lyrics and explored the rich but confusing meanings of American colloquialisms which crop up in the songs of groups ranging from the Pet Shop Boys to Freddie Mercury, while on the floor of the kitchen next door young Olga, sensible girl, snored softly.

Perhaps Galina was a Proustian at heart because at about seven she fell asleep. By then Olga was awake and after a breakfast of tea and biscuits she took me down to the main road and hailed a taxi for me, an official yellow cab this time.

'Have a good day!' said Olga, and waved me out of sight.

The taxi driver was an opera buff devoted to the artistry of the Great Caruso, Beniamino Gigli and Mario Lanza, whom he celebrated by singing snatches from his favourite arias. However his musical tastes were wide-ranging.

'Sixteen tons', he sang, 'and what do you get?'

Only after he had repeated it a couple of times did I understand that this was in the nature of a riddle. I sang back, 'Another day older and deeper in debt.'

This delighted him so much we almost left the road. 'You come from America? England?'

'Africa.'

'You speak good English, for an African.'

He went on laying out his cultural counters for me. 'I read Graham Greene, *Our Man In Havana*, very good. And Alan Sillitoe. I am learning. People cannot go on being stupid.'

His views on the new political changes in the Soviet Union were pungent. He did not believe in them. The reasons for his disbelief were unexpected. Rumour had it, he told me, in fact his brother had it on good authority from a friend, that Mr Gorbachev had built a mansion on the Black Sea which cost twelve million roubles.

'Is this some kind of Jewish perestroika?' he demanded, and then added in a pointed, melodious afterthought, singing the lines in his light, attractive baritone, 'St Peter don't you call me, 'cause I can't go. I owe my soul to the company store.'

Back at my hotel I paid him and added a dollar tip. He rolled the note and passed it beneath his nose like a big cigar.

'In God we trust – and the dollar!'

About hotels, my linguist friend Valentin, usually so knowledgeable in all matters, was quite wrong. It is hardly surprising he knew so little about hotels for foreigners. Foreigners know that Russians have trouble travelling to foreign countries, but they are seldom aware that they have great difficulty even in visiting foreign friends in local hotels. Visitors who do not carry either special permission or a purloined hotel card, or who are not prepared to bribe the doorman, are turned away with a brusqueness that everywhere characterises the attitude of petty officials in shops, offices, airports and hospitals when dealing with members of the public. Shoppers, travellers, pedestrians and drivers exist so that the favoured classes may tell them what to do. The 'insolence of office' is not in the Soviet Union a term of abuse, it is a bonus that goes with the job.

Valentin was devoted to rumour, which in Moscow takes the place of news. In the matter of hotels he told me that the best was somewhere in the centre of the city, built to accommodate the members of the Central Committee of the Communist Party when they came to town. He painted a picture of marble floors, gold taps and ivory balustrades. I went looking for the place more than once, without success. I do not dispute its existence but that hotel has assumed in my mind the same ethereal quality as the President's imperial villa on the Black Sea.

Valentin assured me that the hotel rooms of all foreigners were bugged. Again, I do not dispute this merely because I failed to find any sign of bugging. But if the various rooms I have lived in during my visits to Moscow were electronically surveyed then this suggests a level of efficiency I found nowhere else. If the bugs worked they were exceptional, because nothing else in the hotel did so.

Valentin was speaking out of a long tradition. Eavesdropping has been a confirmed fact of Moscow life noted by independent observers for hundreds of years. One unsympathetic but accurate witness was the Reverend Samuel Collins who served as court physician to the Tsar for nine years in the middle of the seventeenth century. Collins liked very little about the Muscovites, not their manners, their morals or their music, but his testimony is convincing when he reports what a nest of spies the place was. The Tsar routinely sent his secret agents to funerals, feasts and weddings, every meeting was infiltrated and not a whisper passed between his subjects that did not find its way back to the ears of the autocrat. Russian rulers from Ivan the Terrible to his brother in infamy Joseph Stalin have seeded the capital with spies and informers. Rulers and secret police formed a traditional alliance against the people. If Muscovites expect to have their movements controlled and their conversation monitored, how much more likely is it that foreigners should be watched? I am not sure that the expectation is not more effective than the monitoring process itself, and that can only add to its power. A Muscovite, then, will carry special identification if he is to enter a foreign hotel legally; he will also carry a stamp in his passport allowing him to reside and work in Moscow. Called a *propiska*, it resembles the stamp in a 'pass book' which blacks were obliged to carry in South Africa until 1986. When, in the 1930s, Stalin reintroduced the internal passport, the hated symbol of Tsarist control so excoriated by Lenin, he was confirming himself to be an autocrat in the orthodox tradition.

There is much to be said for never leaving the hotel at all in Moscow, which is indeed the fate of many tourists. Having experienced, say, one tour of the Kremlin, shepherded by the disdainful Intourist guide who is inclined to summon her charges in the expanses of Red Square by producing a little red flag, or a scarf or handkerchief, and waving it above her head like an irritable guide mistress, tourists not unnaturally take offence and play truant. They are to be glimpsed back at the hotel, hiding behind the fruit machines or skulking in the lobby when they ought to be shuffling dutifully around the tombs of the Tsars.

The individuality of hotels is quickly exhausted because they are really State guest houses catering for transient foreigners and more important members of the Soviet political hierarchy. Guests comprise three classes: the ebullient and delighted political élite visiting from places like Uzbekistan or Georgia, and happy to be there; Western businessmen, expecting to be businesslike in a city where, until very recently, no business was done, and who soon take on the strained determination of dedicated, but somewhat wary, missionaries; and, finally, the tour groups who wash into the lobbies morning and evening, lost, hungry and bewildered, resembling survivors from some distant disaster, as if the great ship Capital had sunk and they had been pulled out of the drink still wearing their pink shirts and baseball caps and looking like overdressed boat people. They were to be glimpsed, unhappy congregations of puzzled Westerners, milling about outside their separate dining-room, still lost and hungry after breakfast. Their shirts bore legends like *Helsinki My Love* and *California Girl!*, incongruous, zippy notes cruelly at odds with the anxious faces. The early-morning disenchantment of once-innocent tourists, beginning to realise that Moscow was not like Philadelphia, say, or Budapest – worse still it was not even like Leningrad.

'I mean, shit, Leningrad's kind of lovely. Old and lovely. You can tell why the Tsars went there. I'd go there myself if I were a Tsar,' said an American girl, her hair bleached a premature white and a single gold earring shaped like a musical clef swinging angrily from a lobe. 'It's got, well, *views* . . .'

I skirted the group carefully because the Intourist guides who marshall these tourists (motto: 'Our service for your hearts!') have a nasty habit of sweeping up the stragglers and including them in whatever group happens to be passing, East German philatelists or Swiss botanists. They hate untidiness and Western tourists are untidy simply by being there. The Intourist girl addressed her group in the official voice, a note of disdainful command which it is unlikely they had ever heard before, except perhaps in old war movies, the sort of voice that curled around a group of raw recruits, despising their posture and despairing of ever making real tourists out of them.

'Today,' it announced, 'we have Red Square. Anyone who is late misses the bus. Go to the lobby and wait.'

'It wasn't much of a breakfast,' the girl with the gold earring complained, 'just kind of curd, bread and sausage. And I don't eat meat.'

The girl from Intourist looked at her as if she was quite mad. 'Perhaps you would give me the meat that you don't eat.'

The forms of breakfast available in Moscow hotels can be roughly divided into two types. One is the rather oddly described 'Western-style Buffet', and the other is 'Waiter Service'. Both present special problems. In the larger hotels with buffet service, food is arranged on tables to meet a variety of dietary demands ranging from India to Azerbaijan. This method works best for early arrivals. The waiters stand around the walls and watch the guests competing for shrinking supplies; favoured foods go fast and you may find yourself eating more beetroot or vegetable curry than you might usually do at breakfast. The difficulty arises from the laws of supply and demand and it is given to many Western tourists to discover this central problem of the Soviet economy at breakfast time when the system suffers from unexpected overload – when, for instance, a small army of Sikhs, or an orchestra of hungry Romanians, have arrived the night before without notice and sweep through the buffet at first light like the voracious African locust leaving behind only the unidentifiable delicacies of the lesser-known Soviet Republics for the next wave of guests who find they have arrived too late. And too late is too late, for what is gone cannot be replaced and what is left cannot be identified, and the silent waiters look on from their positions around the room with expressions of militant unconcern, anxious only to clear away and start setting the tables for lunch.

If it is the food which disappears in the Western-style buffet breakfast, then at meals with 'waiter service' it is the waiters who vanish. But this is preferable because it means service is certain at least once even if it is never repeated, since the tables have been laid with all that is to be expected the night before and the guest is directed with iron courtesy towards his rations. The waiter service breakfast is usually reserved for individual tourists, businessmen paying the penal rates charged by Moscow hotels for single guests. Private arrangements, paradoxically, are considered to be morally better than the group tour. Westerners in Moscow often constitute the single most powerful argument against the capitalist system. If you wish to warm to the ideals of socialism you have only to spend an hour or two late at night in a foreign currency bar in any of the hotels, where citizens of the hard-currency countries, Finns, Germans, Italians and English, form a small froth floating upon a surface of booze. It is a bit like a fish farm: the spawn below the surface of the pool will eat anything tossed in their direction – or anyone. The overworked bartender hates them, you can see it, but his job is to take their hard currency. And the legless patrons are contemptuous of him, but they need his booze. It is a mutually profitable and deeply unhappy relationship.

The severe shortage of hotel rooms means that you go where you are sent. Price has something to do with it but however much you pay, as with so many other things, choice is strictly limited (if there is choice at all) and shortage is the mother of discovery. It may even be the father of democracy – Soviet style. Valentin liked to quote his father on this subject. 'Who says we don't have democracy? If you don't like standing in this queue, you are free to choose another.'

Since the language of tourism is naturally optimistic and assumes a global consistency, it is one of the chief discoveries of visitors to Moscow to find in the matter of hotels, as in so much else, a distance between words and the realities they so often conceal. The major hotels of Moscow strive to assert differences of character and atmosphere. They range from the 'modern' International Hotel on the Moskva River to the grimly steepled Ukraina. The International is a rather sinister building erected as a joint venture by Soviet and American developers and it is accompanied by its alter ego, the International Trade Centre, an identical building standing beside it. It is as if these twin towers were erected not to celebrate the pleasure but to warn against the pitfalls, of trade and tourism. However, the effect is mild when compared with the baleful aura of the Ukraina, an immense pile which stands across the river and which is the Soviet equivalent of the sort of building King Kong scaled. Tourists returning to the Ukraina after a hard day's sightseeing may be forgiven for believing that they may be suffering from delusions because there appear to be buildings like it all over Moscow. They are right. This form of architecture is called Stalin Baroque by some, new Soviet Rococo by others, and its disfiguring effects are found across the city. It is an architectural language of gigantic statements and brutal flourishes, immense spaces suitable for military parades, vulgar arches and triumphal spires. Seven of these architectural follies were erected in Moscow in the form of a huge heptagon: two are hotels, two ministries, one is an apartment block and one is part of Moscow University up on the Lenin Hills (formerly the Sparrow Hills). The inspiration behind these mammoth monuments – some distance behind them – is possibly the towers of the Kremlin, in particular the Saviour's Tower, most handsome of the towers set in the Kremlin wall.

The old National Hotel predates the Revolution and retains a hint of its former charm. At least the fabric of the building is still in place. The Metropole, where so many important Bolsheviks stayed immediately after the Revolution when Lenin transferred the capital from Petrograd back to Moscow, has been closed for years for 'refurbishment'.

More recent additions include the gigantic Rossiya, the Intourist and the Cosmos Hotels, which wear their modernity like a rather loose disguise, forever slipping to show (whether they boast French restaurants or fruit machines) that they are also places of reeducation and quarantine. Even the Belgrade, bleak and unpretentious, shows the same tendency to schizophrenia. There are not one but two of them, anonymous grey twins on either side of the street: Belgrades I and II. But to attend to the surface is to miss the delights of Moscow: floor ladies, apprentice muezzin and vanishing waiters.

In the hotel of the apprentice muezzin, where I often stayed, the dining-room for private guests lay hidden behind heavy glass doors, curtained against tour groups, and guarded by the maître d'hotel. Admittance was strictly monitored. One paused at the maître's table just inside the door and waited for permission to be seated. A small luminous digital clock pulsed uneasily on the wall, the minutes moving uncomfortably, each passing with a little tremor as if the clock suffered from the electronic equivalent of a facial tic. After identification by room key or hotel card, the maître called the usher, an alpine crag of a man with shining black hair and wearing a black tie and dress-shirt, who combined the looks of a wrestler with those of the mute who once led Victorian funeral processions. Marching along in his wake it was difficult not to be impressed by the dignity of his tread and the gravity of his demeanour. Guests were forcefully directed by the mute to any vacant chair at a crowded table. This brought out the worst in fellow diners who behaved like the creatures at the Mad Hatter's tea party, spreading themselves over as many chairs as possible and pretending there was *no more room*! Such breakfast scenes remain in the memory: importers of silicon chips, salesmen of lathes and chairmen of portable phone companies quoted on the Hong Kong stock exchange behaving exactly like characters from *Alice in Wonderland*. The waiters ignored these little tableaux, set out food on the tables and then, one by one, vanished. We all stared hard at the two pink sausages, sliced cheese, bread and strawberry jam in little plastic pouches which would not yield except after a tremendous struggle. Old hands knew that the seal across the mouth of the plastic pouch gave way without warning. Newcomers usually carried traces of this strawberry paint about for days, the sort of paint inclined, as they say, 'to run'.

Anger will not work. A waiter taught me that; he recommended coming at things from 'other angles'. I went down to breakfast one morning and he was waiting for me wearing a disconsolate distracted look of the ambitious dreamer who is still far from his goal. I asked for eggs. He offered the information that his name was Victor, with a 'c' he said, 'as in Capitalism.' I was trying to be a tourist. He was pretending to be a waiter, but he really wanted to be a stockbroker's clerk; he longed to deal in junk bonds, he wished to live in a condominium. He was supposed to help the guests to breakfast but he was actually in training as a currency dealer. A young man in a faded red jacket and eyes well into middle-age, his moustache looked as if it had been drawn on with a burnt match. Two American nuclear test-ban inspectors at the next table, making the best of a breakfast of beetroot and chillies, lamented the day they had left Atlanta. One glance at the buffet table told me that the exotic locusts from the distant republics had just swept through and all they had left was a little pink cabbage, a lot of butter and sticky exhausted lake beds where the jam had been. Victor said to me, 'Excuse me, you want to exchange currency?'

'Eggs,' I said, 'eggs are what I'd prefer, Victor.'

'I give you a very good rate.'

'I don't want to talk about money. I don't want to exchange currency. Eggs, or even an egg.'

'Or if you like I'll give you caviar.'

'Please sit down, Victor,' I said.

'Well if you don't want roubles and you don't want caviar, what do you want?' Victor sat down happily.

'You want to make a deal? Very well. I will give you money, dollars, if you explain to me how this restaurant works. How this hotel works. How life here in general works.'

Victor thought about it. He looked at me for a long time and then he said, 'Russia is a riddle wrapped in a mystery hidden in an enigma.'

'Eggs, Victor,' I said wearily. 'Don't give me Churchill, give me eggs. Or give me facts. Tell me on what principle this place operates. What are you doing here? What are these other waiters doing here? What are all these rooms for? Why is there no breakfast?'

Victor looked pleased. 'You recognise my quotation! You're well-read.'

'I'm hungry.'

Victor looked owlish. 'Under perestroika I can say we are reading more than ever. And truly I think things have been better since we were allowed to read authors who were forbidden. Yes, in that direction I can say things have improved.'

2

What Do You Read?

The newly liberated intellectuals are free to talk, and what they talk about is 'democracy'. Indeed there is so much talk of it that the discussion might almost be mistaken for the thing itself. The innocent abroad might believe that the Party is relaxing its dictatorship and allowing power to flow to the people. Well then, is everybody in charge, or is no one in charge? Or, as the case of long-dreamt-of reforms in South Africa suggests, is the old firm still in business and simply trading under new names? It is in words and their uses that some clue to understanding is to be sought.

The great central planning bodies for agriculture, industry, construction and the arts are objects of contempt and derision. By decree of the Central Committee of the Communist Party, these mammoths are declared outmoded and have been commanded to put in train programmes by which they will be transformed into modern businesses, subject to strict cost accounting. In other words the men who have created the old, centrally planned, philosophy have been told to hasten its destruction. It is a tall order and the vested interests thus instructed to reform themselves add to the difficulties of understanding what is going on by fruitfully complicating the problems of interpretation. Such problems may be traced to the use of what is called Aesopian language, the language of fables once so essential in dangerous times; a glancing, laconic, allusive, melancholic pattern of reference which proceeds by hints, winks, delicate codes, historical analogies. One sign of genuine novelty in the Soviet Union is the breakdown of Aesopian language which is increasingly dispensed with the further one moves from the centres of power, from the Party, its organs, its bureaucrats, its closed circles of favoured ones. Even some of these are at last discovering the joys of plain speaking, though the ministries, now commanded to reform themselves, are still locked into the old language. Take, for instance, the Ministry of Housing Materials, a contradiction in terms since there are never enough houses and the materials out of which they are constructed fail and falter as you look at them. The existence of the Ministry's very name has become a damaging, cruel, embarrassing joke. In these reforming times when people may speak their minds, an economist suggests in a Moscow newspaper that the Ministry of Housing Materials will soon start transferring its functions of command to leaseholders, who will take over the responsibility for ensuring that such precious, fugitive materials be used efficiently and profitably. He does not say so directly, but the implication is that, as a result of the new thinking, the wretched Ministry, if it does its job properly, will gradually cease to exist.

Down the road, in the Onega Café on Gorky Street, Igor, a young construction worker, is less delicate about the Ministry. 'It should disappear. It can't improve itself, it can only remove itself.' For years many workers like Igor have said such things at home and on the shop floor. Indeed the genuine novelty of perestroika is the way in which the careful, guarded language of Central Committee directives is beginning to resemble some of the things many workers have said privately for decades.

Let the Central Committee speak for itself, as it did in its manifesto for the 1989 elections: 'Big changes are maturing and developing in the economy. Cost accounting and self-financing, cooperation and lease, multiple forms of socialist property are becoming part and parcel of our lives.' Igor holds up his bottle of Czech beer and drops it to the floor where it smashes. The men in anoraks and fur hats do not turn around. 'It's simple,' says Igor. 'The bottle was finished. All we have to do is sweep up the pieces.'

Meanwhile, back at the Ministry of Housing Materials there was consternation and some anger at the suggestion that it might abolish itself. The mammoth declines to cooperate in its own extinction. It issued a statement taking 'certain economists' to task for making the indelicate suggestion. Certainly it was going to delegate its responsibilities, it was amongst the warmest champions of 'our perestroika', but it intended to retain its power to 'administrate'.

A seemingly decisive frankness is part of the new speaking and it often seeks to disguise the truth. Thus, after I told the assistant editor of one of the largest literary magazines that books were routinely banned in South Africa and even, from time to time, in England, he informed me with bland effrontery that, 'we never ban books here any longer'. Grouped around us, listening, were his editorial staff, whose gracious silence spoke volumes. The day before, I had talked to a publisher hoping for permission to bring out something, anything, by Solzhenitzyn. And the day before that, I had listened to an official from Glavlitt, the official censorship agency, telling me which books were seized at the borders: these included anything published by Russian presses abroad; magazines known for their anti-Soviet bias, among which was the 'notorious' *Index on Censorship*; religious propaganda; books by rehabilitated authors such as Pasternak and Gumylov published by foreign presses; magazines, papers and journals containing caricatures of Soviet politicians; any book in fact which the censor finds undesirable and deems offensive.

'For years I tried to get my novel published and the censor stopped it,' a writer explained. 'He made a speech and vowed that my book would never see the light of day while he was around. Well, a little time ago, it was published and, do you know what? – the censor is still around. He doesn't do all the old things, checking references to see if you've mentioned forbidden details like the salary of an airline pilot, or the health of the minister. Today the censor is adapting to changing times: he is regulating the reading matter for the public. He is still very busy doing things. But all I ask him to do is to disappear!' But the censor, it would seem, now quick to deplore censorship, is also determined to preserve his power 'to administrate'.

Certainly more people than ever are reading; there are more books available than ever before. Sociologists in the Soviet Union keep predicting that, as electronic entertainments like television and rock music and video games burgeon, the hunger for reading will begin to abate. Indeed that seems a reasonable suggestion when you witness the crowds of young people down on the Leningrad Railway Station in the middle of Moscow. Video hunting is most popular: a game in which you point your rifle and fire at a cross-section of the animal kingdom ranging from stags to rabbits, and the animals expire with a peculiar little electronic squeal which the young hunters seem to find irresistible. Upon his giant plinth in the centre of the concourse Lenin averts his eyes. In the USSR, perhaps only in the USSR, the video hunters are also readers.

And anyway, the fact is that such amusements remain the province of the few, and while this persists reading will continue to be the private passionate entertainment and consolation of millions. Moscow also houses delicate, acerbic researchers into books and their strange powers, amongst the most perceptive of whom are found at the aptly named Institute of the Book. My favourite observer possessed a delicate and dangerous wit, that lethal but rather beautiful Moscow intelligence which enjoys testing arguments at sword point, combined with a dry, down-beat humour which fetches upon absurdity with grim relish.

'Yes,' said the man from the Institute of the Book, 'there are more books than ever available now, and young people are reading eagerly, though I suspect they do so increasingly for social reasons, for fashionable motives and through a desire to draw real literature into pop culture.'

A prime example was Mikhail Bulgakov's *The Master and Margarita*, a novel which is hugely popular among Moscow high-school students who see it as a kind of cultural totem. The flat described in the novel has become a mecca to which pilgrims flock – indeed, such were the throngs of sightseers at one stage that the police and the KGB put the place off limits and barred the door. The wall beside the stairway to Bulgakov's former apartment is daubed with images and symbols, witches and hangmen and intimate pledges of devotion to the dead author and his still lively, satanic creations; a recognition, I suspect, of how deeply the novel is appreciated because it offers the kind of freewheeling fantasy young people know in their bones will infuriate the authorities. 'Reader!' cries Bulgakov. 'Follow me!' And they do. Contemplating the phenomenon of Bulgakov (and there are many examples of this extra-literary devotion) you feel that book hunger is not simply based on a love of reading, it has its roots in passion, unhappiness and dreams; books bring consolation, forgetfulness, and peace, but they can also wage war.

'Yet although there has been some movement in favour of more editorial freedom,' the man from the Institute of the Book looks politely at the ceiling, 'there is no question of giving the people what they want.'

Two factors conspire to limit the access of readers to the books they wish to read. First, there are the usual shortages – of paper, for example. And with three hundred thousand public libraries in the Soviet Union, and conventional print-runs amounting to some fifty thousand copies, there are never enough books to go around. But it is official obtuseness which is still the main impediment standing between readers and the text.

The right to publish in the Soviet Union depends upon permission from above. Such permission is granted to State publishing houses by a body known as the State Publishing Committee. In the new climate of openness it was decided that this committee would be enriched by the addition of ordinary readers, who would be invited to attend meetings and make suggestions. Books would then be chosen for publication by an ad hoc committee of officials and members of the public, known as 'leaders' and 'readers'. As a reward for useful suggestions, a lucky reader would be allowed to select a title for publication, which in effect meant choosing a bestseller.

At the outset many readers took a keen interest in this new, democratic arrangement. Among their very first suggestions was the call that the official members of the State Publishing Committee should retire. If the State could not afford to pay their pensions then the readers offered to come up with the money themselves. But the members of the committee declined to sacrifice themselves in the service of literature, and the co-opted readers began to have grave doubts about the new openness; doubts which seemed to be borne out when the publishing chiefs responded to their suggestions for several new titles by calling for opinion polls to test the reading public's demands. The man from the Institute of the Book smiled sweetly. 'We then embarked on asking a series of questions to which we already knew the answers . . .'

This is a form of playing with the reader. So are the opinion polls; it can take three years of study to obtain results which have been obvious from the start. But sometimes this research does serve a purpose. The decision to publish Anatoly Rybakov's huge best-selling novel of Stalinist times, *The Children of the Arbat*, was reached after arguments in the Central Committee of the Communist Party, when the publishers produced the poll evidence to show that most readers were in favour of releasing the book, which was written more than twenty years ago.

The taste these days is for Russian writers and in particular for those who were persecuted, expelled or murdered by Stalin, those who wrote political memoirs of the thirties, of the Great Purges, of the labour camps, memories of the age of blood and ice. The feeling is that such writers continued to express, in secret, the spirit of democracy through the dark years of the thirties and forties. They showed that freedom, even if it existed nowhere else, might be found in the imagination, that the mind was a free country where one could travel without passport or permission. 'Russian readers', says the man from the Institute, 'are reclaiming their past. That's why a book like *The Children of the Arbat* could be reprinted tomorrow in a further edition of five million copies and they would sell out immediately. The poetess Anna Akhmatova sells in editions of one million copies.'

However, there are writers who are out of favour, those who date from the stagnant era of the seventies and early eighties, worthy hacks, not particularly bad writers, who toed the Party line and rejoiced in an era when, in the delicious phrase of the man from the Institute, 'homogeneity was more convenient'. They wrote the sorts of novels then officially sanctioned and published in editions of many millions. They employed what Muscovites call the 'prose of secretaries' and constructed from it a 'literature for generals'. Such writers are not pleased by the triumphant return of Nabokov and the resurrection of Pasternak, and undoubtedly suffer by comparison.

What Do You Read?

Not all books most sought after are by liberals or old social realists. There is, too, a literature of the countryside, the 'village writers', defiantly rural, passionate ecologists, but also nationalist and anti-Semitic in tone, fiercely anti-Western, mysogynist and sentimental. Among other things, these writers have a horror of aerobics, refer to rock and roll as 'spiritual Aids', and take a view of women that St Paul would have applauded.

None of this is to suggest that these writers, good, bad or reactionary, are freely available. You soon realise that in the matter of books, bookshops are not the place to find them, since shops exist largely to remind you of what you cannot buy. (To counter the shortage a cooperative has been established which brings owners of precious and desirable books together, for a small consideration – a sort of literary dating agency, where the reader is introduced to the author of his dreams. Better by far than going shopping for them.) The biggest bookshop in Moscow, on Kalinin Prospekt, is known as the House of Books and it is run on penitentiary lines. In the foreign section you may buy copies of *How To Be Polite in Japanese*, but no contemporary writers are available; even the classics like Pushkin are in short supply – a fact in which the shop assistants take fierce pride. However, congregated in the entrance to the shop are a group of young men who look at first glance like mafiosi. In fact they are black marketeers offering copies of books – not forbidden books, you understand, but unobtainable classics, Bulgakov, Pasternak, Mandelstam, which they will let you have at a price. With what agonies must Russians investigate the curious mystery of supply. And supply will remain a mystery in the Soviet Union for some time to come, I imagine, while demand will be painfully apparent in the queues on every street.

The existence of people like the man from the Institute of the Book, and others whom I met on my visits to Moscow, is the source of many consolations. Their lonely independence of mind makes up an internal resistance against which the 'new thinking' must test itself. All the talk of reform, the promises and pronouncements which go under the name of perestroika, make their way into the minds of such people and are bathed in acid until all base metal dissolves or discloses itself. They are exceptionally sensitive to the presence of the lie, having spent lifetimes learning to recognise it. Now they have cooled to an icy scepticism and they will test to destruction all advertisements and reports of political virtue and offers of reform. And they do not need much to go on, they do not have to see the whole manifesto, or even the entire promise, a fragment will do, a word, a phrase. The difficulty for those in charge of the new dispensation will be to recruit such people to their cause. They have been left out for so long that it has become a source of bitter pride; the things they most wanted, precision, accuracy, plain speaking, have been forbidden to them; they sit on the far edge of things having the gift (it is their single reward) of smelling out the fraudulent a mile away. Whether such people can be reconciled with the governing centre is hard to say, but it seems unlikely while those in charge remain a law to themselves. For me this cold yet passionate integrity is heroic; it is also the only valid measure of present political changes and it is to the credit of Gorbachev and others that such changes allow such people to speak.

The true achievement of glasnost and perestroika has been the slow opening up of language; a closer relationship between words and their meanings is being encouraged for the first time since the Revolution. The brutal, armoured prose of Party documents, closely identified with Stalin but continued by the leaders who succeeded him, is giving way to a new openness of expression. Until very recently, official lies endlessly repeated constituted the 'truth'. Now Party documents, at the very highest levels, seem to be struggling towards an attempt to communicate, not yet the truth, perhaps, but half-truths at least, and, considering the distance to be travelled, that is a good start.

Consider Leonid Batkin's brilliant analysis (published in *Moscow News*) of Stalin's official prose style, taking as an example his speech to the 18th Party Conference in 1939, at the height of the Terror. Batkin cites the following gem: 'The issue of bold and timely promotion of new and young cadres is of particular importance. I think that our men still lack complete clarity concerning that issue. Some believe that the old cadres should mainly be chosen when selecting personnel. Others would orient themselves more towards the young cadres. I think that both the former and the latter are mistaken.' Batkin vividly conveys the elements of Stalin's style: 'The grandeur of a self-consciously ponderous shaman, the rhetorical devices of a half-educated seminarian, murderous bureaucratic jargon . . . a menacing tone and meagreness of expression.' Its logic was that it contained nothing logical; it could not be understood but it inspired terrified belief; those who heard it knew it must mean something simply because it had been spoken. Had Stalin declared that the Volga flowed into the Caspian Sea, Batkin says, 'Everyone would have been struck by the accuracy and simplicity of the truth.' Stalinism was an atmosphere, it was the air people breathed. They knew what he intended before he said it. When at the Congress in 1949 Stalin spoke not a single word, his silence impressed his audience as forcibly as any speech, and Batkin concludes that 'the absence of text seemed to have as much meaning as a regular text'.

Batkin extends his merciless analysis by emphasising that Stalin's anti-logic did not simply emerge from nowhere but drew on the models of earlier Party leaders (by implication Lenin) who were, after all, responsible for taking the meaning of words into Party ownership. Having assumed this proprietorial role it is hardly surprising that the Party is now firmly associated in the minds of many people with the bankruptcy and fraudulence of all official political pronouncements. An injured awareness of this near-fatal association between Party policies and great wretchedness may be seen in the almost tender note to be found in the 1989 Party Manifesto for the elections to the Congress of People's Deputies. It is a fascinating document – not only for the words it employs, but for its tone of voice: it speaks in the accents of a shepherd to his flock, and one has to keep reminding oneself that this is no papal encyclical, it is the voice of the Central Committee of the Communist Party of the Soviet Union. 'Comrade electors, the very idea of perestroika was born of concern for the individual. The pivot of the entire socio-economic policy of the CPSU is to raise the well-being and to improve the life of the Soviet people. The vital needs of the people are close and understandable to the Party, and it is persistently working for Soviet people to live better in the coming years.'

The movement from murderous discussion of the suitability of 'cadres', in Stalin's reign, to the solicitude of the Central Committee towards 'comrade electors' and on, still further, to the clear demands of a bold critic of the government, Andrei Sakharov, reveals a slow process of clarifying the language. In Sakharov's election manifesto, language becomes the vehicle of real political debate which seems shocking for being fresh. He calls for personal freedoms, for the abolition of the internal passport, and his demands seem bold simply because they sound so natural. 'Each person should be paid according to his work. All restrictions on the size of one's earning must be eliminated. The size of salaries of all officials must be published. All public foundations should publish annual financial accounts.' By measuring Party prose against the clarity of Sakharov's demands and the brevity of their expression, one can see how far the careful kindliness of the Central Committee has still to go.

Yet none of this goes far enough for the factory worker, the fitter, or the steelman who stood beside me in the queue to the ice-cream stall in Gorky Park and said, quite simply, that there was no point in saying anything about 'them' because 'they' were 'dead in the head'. Indeed, it is this violent rejection of 'them' that has so boosted the popularity of Boris Yeltsin. The fact that Yeltsin was once one of 'them' is neither here nor there. When he was Moscow Party boss 'he stirred up the shit', as my friend in the ice-cream queue explained. 'He stood in queues and complained about shortages and told the big-shots to go to hell.' And so when 'they' fired him, Yeltsin's popularity expanded hugely. Rough, tough, vulgar and, above all, pissed off, he was the sort of man you went with to a hockey game; from being one of 'them', he became one of 'us'. He was the people's champion and thus it is not astonishing that those who claim to speak on behalf of the people came to hate and fear him. 'They paid him the greatest compliment,' said the man in the ice-cream queue. 'They began to spread the rumour that he was part Jewish!'

*

What Do You Read?

How, then, to read what is happening? Whom to read? Reports in the papers discuss events which have yet to occur: democracy, freedom, consumer choice, full shelves and the rule of law. Perestroika continues to be written in the future tense, but glasnost means we can talk about it now – or not.

In Moscow people suddenly fall silent in the face of suggestions from Westerners that things are getting better; or lively amusement shot with – what? Pity, perhaps? – shows in their eyes, shaded with a trace of embarrassment. Droll perturbation among friends and strangers is bad enough, but it is the look of pain, even anger, that startles. You learn to avoid giving offence as you learn not to make comments of a suggestive nature in polite company. It has been increasingly difficult for some time to find anyone willing to defend the present system. What is less well known, perhaps, is that it is almost as hard to find people enthusing about the moves towards a new political dispensation, except amongst those responsible for peddling the new ideas. Even the beneficiaries –intellectuals, technocrats, readers – do not display enthusiasm.

Yet the gains are clearly visible in certain quarters. As political controls loosen, more people are joining what may be called the receiving classes, which are badged about with material signs of success: the Japanese video recorder, the Taiwanese telephone chirruping in its wall bracket; tokens and totems; the smudged photostats of last week's Western satellite TV programmes; the Dutch tiles in the kitchen, the drinks trolley loaded with Ararat brandy, Dubonnet and gin. A rather touching habit of sly ostentation is the display of favoured books by standing them front-cover outwards on the shelves; and the habit extends to records, foreign newspapers, even empty wine bottles. They stand proudly in the glassfronted or open display cabinets much prized in the homes of people on the move, an item of furniture Russians call a 'wall'. There is increased access to foreign travel and its vital lubricant, hard currency, the most privileged of all benefits. Yet material gains do not blunt the edge of dissent from, and disagreement with, the inadequacies of the Soviet system, even if they undoubtedly sweeten the lives of the politicians, writers, film-makers and journalists who enjoy them; indeed they often sharpen criticism. The young rock singer who clamps his

British-made steering-wheel lock around the controls of his precious Moskvitch on a Sunday afternoon outside the public sauna and then carefully removes his windscreen wipers (beloved of car thieves and worth their weight in gold) and places them in his Nike sportsbag, is not likely to be very impressed by promises of political reform. He is painfully aware of how far the Soviet Union lags behind other countries in the production of such modern delights. And it is his ability to make the comparison – he may even have been to the West and seen the difference – that distinguishes him from the majority of Muscovites.

Searching for a term to describe this class of people, my friend Valentin, the linguist, considered briefly, only to reject, the term 'petite bourgeoisie'. 'In fact I think you could call them the "petit intelligentsia".' Valentin was an English specialist, he spoke the language with supple authority and idiomatic precision, and he employed to the full the melancholy Russian gift of asking unanswerable questions couched in tones of doleful wonder.

'Don't you think it's interesting,' he remarked, 'that we have in Moscow so many expert linguists, at home in the languages of countries they have never seen and never expect to be allowed to visit?'

Open complaints are not often heard among Muscovites. Instead statements and questions are given a wintery edge, and Valentin rejoiced in the capacity for self-lacerating humour, a sad affection for the absurd. You laughed even as you iced over. His questions were ones to which I had no answers. When I asked questions expecting answers, he laughed. It was a vivid educational experience. Poetic, pessimistic, fiercely nostalgic for the 'true' Russia, he was a faithful yet resolutely disenchanted member of the Party, which he considered to be the greatest obstacle to reform in the Soviet Union today.

'They take a vote. I raise my hand. The motion passes.'

What, I asked, should I read? Whom should I read?

'Read our minds,' he replied. 'No, that is not enriching. Read the city, the faces; read the Metro.'

The Moscow Metro stations, from Marx Prospekt to

Mayakovskaya stations, are a series of people's palaces built in much the same spirit as the Victorians constructed their railway stations, as temples to progress intended to flatter the natives and disconcert the foreigner. The first catacombs of marble, porphyry, bronze, mosaic and steel were quarried in the thirties by Stalin's henchman Lazar Kaganovitch; 70,000 men and women working round the clock. Bulganin the supervisor and Krushchev the foreman together pushed the work through at a terrible cost in human life as well as widescale destruction of great sections of the city, in order to meet the deadline of May 1935 when the first line was to be opened by Stalin. But clean and swift and grand they are, if you forget the ghosts, and for five kopeks you may ride as far as you like. Crowds pour down the wooden escalators, urgent yet not rushed, quick but not eager, alert yet somehow also subdued, a ceaseless descent of the orderly thousands intended to convey how the Soviet State keeps the masses moving. At once palatial and disconsolate, no dirt, colour, danger, distress; no graffiti, no noise and, I'm almost tempted to add, no life. Looking at the silent frozen masses descending I thought of Eliot's description of the crowds flowing over London Bridge: 'I had not thought death had undone so many.'

That was before I learned to look more carefully and closely, before I saw the beggars bestowing a blessing when alms are given – and many people do give, stooping almost furtively to drop a few coins in an outstretched palm, straightening quickly and crossing themselves. And the flower sellers hawking the inevitable red carnations. And the gypsies against whom you are warned to guard your purse. 'May I ask?' the gypsies enquire over and over, mostly receiving emphatic refusals as women clutch their handbags and men gesture angrily.

It was, in a paradoxical way, a sign of life, something that ran counter to the apparent uniformity of it all, one of those revealing spots or blemishes on the apparently bland surface of Moscow life.

Consider, for example, the boy who disobeyed. They sometimes switched off one escalator in the Metro to save power and forbade its use. Down the immobile escalator strode a boy of about twenty. The floor lady at the bottom of the stair rose from her chair in disbelief and began screaming at him. Why did he not use the moving escalator like everybody else? Several hundred obedient commuters moving down the working escalator turned their heads between miscreant and accuser, like crowds at a tennis match, reflecting her surprise but not her rage, watching with expressions of guarded anticipation the boy skipping his way downstairs. The floor lady's threats grew shriller and fiercer. The boy had gone too far to turn back. He kept moving, not bothering to smile or even to look apologetic, or in any way to acknowledge he had heard her cries. Would she invoke some sanction to make him turn back, some special authority for dealing with the flagrant breach of regulations? We waited, she yelled, nothing happened. And we all saw nothing happen, and we knew as we moved sedately down the orthodox stairway that in taking the way you should not take, the boy had shown what others might do after him. He disappeared into the milling crowds on the station. The lady scowled after him and then resumed her chair and her immobile watch at the bottom of the escalators. All who saw it understood. In that wondrously organised, highly policed, subdued and deferential society something had stirred.

When you visit Moscow great play is made of the magnificent underground stations, the cheapness of the fares, the punctuality of the trains, 125 miles of track and being extended all the time. Less common is to be told of the devastation which took place when the Metro was built. The pain such contemplation of past destruction may engender is plain to see in the eyes of an elderly archaeologist when he talks of the Moscow he remembers. There is a dark, almost violent shadow in and around his eyes, as if some form of internal bruising had taken place; he winces when he summons up the ghosts of palaces, churches and houses swept away.

'But we have a beautiful Metro. You've been? I never use it myself. Yes, excuse me, but you see I become physically ill if I go down into the Metro.'

It seemed to me that the temples to progress, the underground stations in their marble and bronze, were alarming in their aggressive architecture but I had never thought of them as sickening.

'But they are, for me. Did you know that there was a shortage of bricks when they built the underground, so many of the ancient Russian villages outside Moscow were demolished and their bricks used to build the stations?'

The old archaeologist traces the roots of destruction back to the Revolution when forces loyal to the provisional government of Kerensky were holed up in the Kremlin and the commander of the Red Artillery began bombarding their position, knowing that, for the purposes of the Revolution, the destruction of ancient monuments was permitted by Lenin. To his credit, Lenin rescinded the instruction shortly after the Bolshevik victory but the pattern was set, and after his death the destruction of historical monuments, churches and other buildings began on a grand scale.

'But it is not just the spaces we have levelled, it is the things we have built there! You've travelled along our Garden Ring?'

The Garden Ring is a road circling Moscow and I knew what he meant; it is notable for its lack of gardens, its almost fatal absence of greenery. Silver birches grow haphazardly between the apartment blocks but flowers are flown in to Moscow from Georgia and gardens are unknown.

'Let me tell you the story of the Church of Christ the Saviour. It is a famous story in Moscow, everyone knows it. As a foreigner perhaps you will also enjoy it. The Church of Christ the Saviour was the biggest in Moscow. It was raised by donations from the people to commemorate the victory over Napoleon and it took over forty years to build. It was completed in 1880. One day Stalin decided to demolish it. The contractors moved in. But the church resisted. Thousands and thousands of people had built it and built it well. The walls withstood the demolishers' attack, they refused to fall down.

'So the job was put in the hands of the Cheka, the secret police, forerunner of the KGB. Strict instructions from the Boss to get rid of it. The Cheka built a fence all the way around it and set dynamite charges. The resulting explosion blew out windows many miles away and the walls at last came down.'

The old archaeologist gave me one of his fierce, bitter smiles. I had seen plans of the building Stalin proposed to replace the church, a vast Palace of Soviets built in the grotesque wedding-cake style of Stalin Baroque, and its many tiers were to have stood three hundred metres high, crowned with a giant statue of Lenin one hundred metres tall. Rumours suggested that his eyes were to cast a bright red beam visible for kilometres, like an ideological lighthouse. But the ziggurat was never built, the ground was too marshy, and in its stead Stalin built a great outdoor swimming pool. On cold nights steam rises from its heated water and in summer the cries of the bathers can be heard in the nearby Kropotkin Square Metro.

'What we have today instead of a church,' said the old archaeologist, 'is a giant baptismal font where all of Moscow goes to bathe but cannot wash away their sins.'

There is a delight in studying old stones and tracing their origins. Stones, says the old man, tell stories, and sometimes they take their revenge.

'Once the destruction of the Church of Christ the Saviour was effected, the bricks from which it had been built became the property of the KGB and some of the bricks were used by their owners to build houses. I got my house from a man with KGB connections who built it in 1931, using stone from the church. It is a curious feeling because as a boy I played on the steps of Christ the Saviour. I can remember the beggars, priest and coats of arms. Now I live in a house which has foundations built from the stone of the church.

'The passion for destruction has been over for a decade or more and the emphasis today is on preservation of what remains. This too brings problems. We save the old buildings, and restore them. Then no one knows what to do with them! And you get some nationalist organisations, fascists, anti-Semites, who resent the salvation of a church if it is to be turned into an office or a gallery. They blame not the developers but the victims. They look for scapegoats. They hold noisy meetings where they blame every-one except themselves for the changes in the city. Especially they blame the Zionists.'

I suggested to the old archaeologist that no one had done more to damage his capital city than Stalin, except perhaps Nero. He looked at me steadily for a moment and then said quietly, 'Ah, please, I must ask you not to underestimate our achievements.'

And what of views of the city, stock views, tourist views; could I read anything into them? Valentin thought not. 'There are no views, and if there were, the pollution from the cars and factories would mask them.' Ignoring his protests I bought a ticket for an Intourist view of the city and found a taxi to take me to the assembly point for the tour, which left at ten o'clock. It was the dead of winter, with an ankle-high wind straight out of Siberia chivvying the snowflakes into dirty white dunes. I chose my driver from the dense mob of furtive men who stamp and steam like cart-horses on the steps of the big hotels. These are freelance operators: when not driving cabs they may be touts, card sharps, pimps and pushers, or all of these together, and they take advantage of the frequent refusals of the drivers of the official yellow cabs to take anyone anywhere at any price. Their cabs are usually battered jalopies with a meter well concealed in a dark corner somewhere beneath the dashboard.

Gennady was young and wild-eyed. Though the temperature was well below freezing, he wore only a light jacket, no scarf and no hat. The lack of headgear should have warned me – always keep your head warm in the Moscow winter, friends warned me – but then, as I was to discover, Gennady and his head had long ago decided to go their own ways. His car was elderly, grey and freezing. Deposits of muddied snow left by the boots of earlier passengers had frozen solid on the bare metal floor. The shy little meter lurking under the dashboard showed twenty roubles. I pointed this out to Gennady. He hit it several times with his fist but the meter never flinched and the price stayed at twenty roubles. Gennady shrugged. 'No problem,' he said, in English. I later discovered these were the only words of English he spoke. He also seemed to speak very little Russian. As we slithered into the traffic on his badly worn tyres, I found myself wondering if Gennady was a real taxi driver. Perhaps he wasn't even a real *fake* taxi driver. Maybe he was some crazy kid who had seen me coming and grabbed one of the cabs that stand by the kerb, engines running on icy mornings. I scribbled our destination on a piece of paper; he raised a thumb. 'No problem!'

I might have taken the Metro. Perhaps I should have taken the Metro. I had been assured when I bought my ticket that the tour collection point was just 'five minutes away'. But that sort of promise is a clear warning in Moscow, where everything takes longer than you think, and so I chose Gennady over the Metro and gave myself a good hour. Catherine the Great was among those who cautioned visitors about the difficulties of getting around. It could take an entire day to cross the city, she complained in her memoirs, adding that it was almost impossible to achieve anything at all in Moscow; it was, she observed, 'the seat of sloth', the place was slovenly, the temper of the people cruel and the temptations to tyranny greater than anywhere else in the world. As I sat back on the uncertain springs I felt she might have sympathised. We inched our way forward in the heavy traffic of Kalinin Prospekt, down towards the Kremlin. A pigeon settled on the bonnet. The appearance of the bird seemed to delight Gennady because he began rapidly flapping his elbows like stubby wings. The pigeon flew away. This seemed an unhappy omen. The pigeon had been to Russians a sacred creature, venerated for its relation to the dove, symbol of the Holy Ghost. I thought for a moment I had been given a glimpse beneath the skin of things, back into that other, older world which the present brutal disposition of Moscow, and so much of Russian life, seeks to disguise; back to the passionate traditional delights of Muscovites which travellers in other ages so deplored: speed, sledges, dwarfs, buffoons, beatings, bears, public executions, drink, churches and chess. In my romantic enthusiasm I put Gennady down as that other specially Russian phenomenon, the holy fool. But only for a moment.

The windscreen had iced over. Gennady took to rubbing the ice with a piece of old newspaper. He managed to clear a circular spyhole about the size of a tennis ball and drove with his nose close to the dirty glass. I was glad I could see nothing of the road ahead. Instead, through the side window, I watched the old men chipping ice on the pavements. Other workers shovelled snow into heaps at the side of the road. A snow plough was moving along the kerb collecting the snow. Another brace of workers sprinkled the swept pavements with sand: one man pulled a little cart on skinny wheels rather like a baby's pram, piled with dark brown sand, while his companion wielded a long-handled spade, digging deeply into the sand and spreading it in a shapely curve with the graceful rhythm of a sower scattering seed, each curve being drawn at regular intervals so that the pavement became a long caterpillar darkly banded, winding between snow dunes. It seemed a form of sidewalk artistry, a craft of the new urban peasantry.

I knew Gennady was lost when he stopped to consult a policeman. Three lines of automobiles were breaking the speed limit in both directions along Kalinin Prospekt and the policeman, in grey coat and fur hat, stood in the middle of the road directing the lethal traffic with his long white truncheon and bright, strident silver whistle. They are big men, the Moscow militia, and so well wrapped in winter that they seem not so much to walk as to lumber. They dominate street corners in glass crow's-nests raised above the heads of the pedestrians, or they walk the white line in the road barking orders at all who come near, twirling their truncheons on leather thongs and looking like huge, irritable majorettes. Famed for their stupidity yet admired for their brave masculinity which makes them heroes of many a novelette, objects of respect and derision, their very size and substance, combined with a kind of furry hauteur, makes them impressive and remote figures. Their bearing and the way they lean backwards to correct centres of gravity locked somewhere deep inside all those layers of insulation, and their winter contours, well wrapped, well fed, heavily superior, means they are not approachable figures. Yet Gennady approached, a pauper out to petition the prince, a Charlie Chaplin tramp in threadbare grey trousers and thin jumper, grinning and dodging the hurtling traffic. (Muscovites have long doted on speed, whether in sleighs, troikas or motor cars; the fun lies in getting there as quickly, and as dangerously, as possible.) Aghast at his progress, the policeman tried to wave him back. Gennady returned the greeting and went on dodging cars. He gained the centre of the road. The policeman cursed him. Gennady studied the falling snow. The tirade over, Gennady folded his hands and asked directions and the white truncheon stabbed the air in an unmistakable gesture of contempt. Minutes later, bald tyres skidding dangerously on the icy road, we set off back the way we had come.

Time was shortening. I leaned across the seat and tapped my watch. Gennady grinned and tapped his fuel gauge which showed an empty tank. Scratch a Muscovite and find a chess player. We pulled into a muddy yard that look like a cross between a car-boot sale and a traffic jam, crowded with trucks, saloons, official limos and even an ambulance driven by a man taking his girlfriend on a jaunt. The snow fell in a gentle hesitant way, very tiny flakes, small as salt. A heavy cloud of petrol and diesel fumes hung over us from engines left running to warm their drivers against the cold, and we all displayed an African patience. The man in charge hid in a little hut: a shy creature, just a pale moon face behind the glass, and sleepy dark eyes, he kept out of sight, like a hermit or a fugitive. But he was friendly enough when approached, though he turned his face from me while we chatted and presented an ear in rather the way a priest does in the confessional.

Petrol was very cheap, just forty kopeks per litre – a few years before it had been even cheaper, costing the same as a bottle of mineral water. The petrol was exchanged for coupons; official drivers were issued with a supply every three months and were expected to make them last. At the end of the year they had to get rid of them fast because the new year's coupons replaced the old and rendered them obsolete. Of course, like everything else, those surplus coupons were negotiable: the owners of private cars, who suffered inconvenience, indignity and the constant attentions of the militia, were always happy to take up any spare. There were whispers that the price of petrol might well increase again but my informant said piously, 'One tries not to believe rumours. Everyone knows price increases must come. But, officially, they won't admit it. There is a rumour that Brezhnev was always in the habit of beginning each meeting of the Politburo by announcing, "Gentlemen, there will be no price reforms." I believe it.'

'Then you do believe in rumours?'

'I must believe in something.'

I recognised where we were when we got lost again, in the merchants' quarter behind St Basil's Cathedral. I recognised from my reading the house of the merchant Dolgov, a Corinthian mansion designed by Bazhenov, who had been all the rage in the eighteenth century. Deeply frustrated because Catherine the Great rejected out every idea he ever offered her, Bazhenov contemplated killing himself. I knew how he must have felt. We moved next to the sugar-cube, seventeenth-century Church of St Nicholas, built by the regiment of musketeers commanded by Colonel Pyzhov, every single man of which was executed by Peter the Great in Red Square after an abortive palace revolt. Then with a skating U-turn we drew up outside the great house which once belonged to a rich merchant called Igumnov. It had been designed by the architect Posdeev but Igumnov hated it and refused to pay. Posdeev took his revenge in the manner most appropriate to a spurned architect and hanged himself inside the mansion. I doubt Gennady knew that. After his death Lenin's brain was taken to the house for examination. In the postwar period the house became the residence of the French Ambassador. I doubt Gennady knew that either because he leapt from the car and ran to the policemen guarding the front gate. The sight of a hatless, coatless man with wild eyes running towards the French Ambassador's house excited the guards and a short sharp exchange took place. When Gennady got back into the car his nose was bleeding. It seemed to help. After that we found our way, Gennady's nose to his tiny tunnel of vision, calling out the street names as we passed; once we executed a rapid reversal manoeuvre which I suspect changed forever the life of the bus driver coming up behind us at speed, but we arrived at the address on my piece of paper with a couple of minutes to spare.

It was a short, nondescript muddy street. Two great empty Intourist coaches stood at the kerb, engines rumbling, drivers dozing at the wheel. Gennady raised a thumb and tapped his meter. It showed forty roubles, a small fortune.

'But that includes the twenty roubles already on your meter when we started. We've driven around half of Moscow and this place can't be more than ten minutes from my hotel! I won't pay!'

Gennady pointed to my piece of paper and to the street name and to one of the Intourist coaches which had begun suddenly moving off, broad-beamed and hippopotamic; then he pointed to his watch: ten o'clock. He had me and he knew it.

I paid him. 'You're an incompetent swine and I ought to kill you.'

'No problem,' Gennady beamed.

If I hadn't been there myself I would not have believed it. I went there myself and still did not believe it. Ah Moscow, Moscow! The quiet, rather dingy, little street and single remaining bus whose driver, without opening his eyes, told me he knew nothing about a tour of the city. Nothing. I began running up and down the stairs of every building. On each landing, a floor lady; from each floor lady fresh advice – try upstairs, downstairs, next door. Pierced by arches once used by carriages, the buildings were honeycombed with offices – some overlooked the street, others contemplated a sandy, snow-swept courtyard at the rear. It was now after ten, too late for my tour, but some mad perversity kept me running. The few glimpses of what passes for Moscow office life were instructive. People arrived in a steady stream but they moved slowly as if unwilling to get into the office with its harsh strip neon overhead and flimsy partition walls, the smell of sawdust and plastic, and none of the hum and bustle you expect in a real office. I listened to the long silences of people arriving and taking off boots, coats, hats and gloves. In despair I went back into the street and woke the driver dozing in the big empty coach. 'Around the corner,' he advised, 'they'll put you right.' And he went back to sleep.

Around the corner was Gorky Street. Now I knew Gorky Street, but coming at it from the angles Gennady had chosen, the city seemed to have tilted on its head. I discovered I had been scurrying around the backyard of the enormous Intourist Hotel. Down the street was the giant black equestrian statue of Prince Dolgoruky, Moscow's founder, wearing his winter cloak of thick snow. Suddenly the world fell into place. The Intourist Hotel laid claim to a certain modernity, a Coke machine, a small enclosure aglow with unattended one-arm bandits; wall to wall the machines stood, humming and winking to themselves as if this were a holy cult, some lonely meeting of a tribe of electronic Indians. The Intourist Hotel even boasted a special department offering tours of the city of Moscow – I was home!

The lady at the tours desk was brisk.

'No, not here. This is simply where we sell the tickets. You must go out of the hotel again. Behind the hotel you will find a yard. In the yard you will find your guide.'

'But there is no guide!'

'If there is a tour there must be a guide.' And her wave, directing me back the way I had come, indicated that no further conversation was possible.

I knew it was hopeless, I had been there before and there was no guide. But I went grimly out again into the snowy yard all the same and I climbed the stairs in all the buildings I had not yet visited. I moved like a ghost through the dusty light of shabby offices; I heard how the rusty swing doors, which operate on ancient springs, emit almost human squeals whenever the door opens to admit another reluctant office worker. It was the only nearly human sound I heard. Some of the buildings dated back to the eighteenth century, with stone floors, high ceilings, dark wooden doors, their noticeboards advertising every conceivable variety of trade union life, the massed slogans unexpectedly bright in dim interiors which reminded me of the mote-laden light of waiting rooms in lesser Victorian railway stations. None of the disconsolate office workers paid much attention to me. I had the impression that if I'd sat down at a desk and begun working no one would have noticed for weeks, perhaps years.

I went back to the Intourist Hotel. A new lady had taken the chair, a kindly woman who listened to my story. Her smile was broad and friendly. She even patted my arm. 'I have very good news for you. Fortunately your journey has not been in vain. You see, today is Tuesday. And we have no tours on Tuesday.'

I was rather disconsolate for some days after the tour I never took and I found myself haunting other transport systems, the Metro the major stations, the airport. Valentin enjoyed the story of my tour. 'This is the first step to learning that you can never understand Moscow,' he said. 'As Tyutchev wrote, you have to *believe* in it.' Then he pointed out that the places I had later fixed on to visit were all points of departure. Perhaps, secretly, I wished I had never come to Moscow? It was a very common feeling, he said, there were many Muscovites who felt like that. It was a sign of feeling at home, this desire to leave, to be desperate to take off for somewhere else. Possibly, on a deeper level, this fascination with terminals and jumping-off points hinted at a darker form of depression, perhaps even an attraction towards self-destruction? Again, he assured me, suicidal tendencies were widespread.

'As you know, our telephone system is very good. It costs a few kopeks to call across the city. No time limit. But for one section of society, calls are free: the terminally depressed. For them there is a helpline. Do you think the government is trying to tell us something?'

And I read the railway stations – especially that great triangle of departure comprising three stations, the Leningrad, the Yaroslavl and Kazan. I particularly liked the Yaroslavl, not least because it horrified Valentin.

'What on earth can you possibly want there? It is a picture of hell. It is not a suitable subject.'

People in transit forget themselves. The people in these stations had no time to wonder how they looked to people who looked at them. They had no experience of being looked at, and they stayed in one place long enough for the observer, the maker of sketches, to form an impression. They stayed in the place for days, sometimes, in a kind of professional coma of those who expect a lengthy delay.

At the modern Leningrad Station people always seem to be arriving; the smarter provincials from the former capital go stepping briskly through the echoing concourse. It was at this station that Lenin arrived on 11 March 1918, after transferring back to Moscow the government of the Soviet Union, the new Revolutionary state, in love with the future and harnessed to history. As the new Revolutionary government took possession of the Kremlin, ancient fortress of the Tsars, Lev Trotsky, with a hint of relief, declared that the new rulers harboured no desire for vengeance, they had, he claimed, nothing of Hamlet in them. Time was quick to prove him wrong. A huge, rather brutal bust of Lenin upon a tall, bleak, grey column watches over the modern arrivals.

Across the road is the Yaroslavl Station from where the Trans-Siberian trains pull out for Vladivostok over nine thousand kilometres away. Not much happens in the Yaroslavl to distract the waiting travellers. Then one day, someone was making a movie. A young man, upon whom fancy cameras hung like six-guns on a Trappist monk, was pointing a large and expensive Sony at another young man dressed to look, I suspected, like a young peasant up from the country. Wearing a black suit, open-necked white shirt and an old hat, and carrying a large bag, he was required to walk towards the camera again and again, whilst spreading out on either side of the camera in two wings were attendants, supporters, technical back-up, that constellation of bodies film-makers require. Passengers waiting for their train for Vladivostok stared with undisguised fascination at these scenes from a day in the life of young metropolitans: the jeans, the aggressive sub-Western swagger, the cameras, the endless and seemingly needless repetition. The next day the film-makers had vanished. A few passengers demonstrated for new arrivals what they had missed. Then everyone settled back in their chairs and it was Sunday again in coma city.

Outside the Kazan Station across the way, the porters in handsome blue uniforms blow on their hands and stamp their feet in the snow, sufficient to themselves, a club, a community, an order, cheerful, big men, chatting and smoking. What they do not seem to be doing is carrying bags. Hawkers, hookers, porters, photographers, babies, men with portable loudspeakers advertising the pleasures of Moscow tours in the ancient buses which stand at the kerb, belching blue smoke; left-luggage lockers, lost-luggage kiosks; food for the journey; six eggs and half a yard of sausage wrapped in cellophane and selling like hot cakes; there are no hot cakes but there is plenty of ice-cream, though the temperature is well below freezing; soldiers, seamen, conmen, gypsies, beggars and little old ladies wrapped as tightly as the parcels they carry, dozing. The public address system makes a soft, remote, alien purr seemingly unrelated to the people, and they are the people, the *narod*, the real thing and their role is to wait, watch, wonder, and do as they are told. The faces of those setting out seem to point in the direction of their expectations, waiting under the great curving concrete roof and massive chandeliers in the pistachio gloom of the massive concourse. Upon orange plastic chairs the patient thousands sit for hours, perhaps for days. Mothers rock their babies, to and fro they swing like pendulums. Where else should they wait? A mother who has brought her child to Moscow for medical treatment, for instance, cannot stay in a hotel – there are none to cater for that sort of thing. So she will sit here until the time comes to catch the train back to Tashkent.

In the slanting snow, on platform no. 2, the train for Tashkent was preparing to receive its passengers. At the door of each carriage stood the guard carrying a flag and wearing a large round fur hat. She had spent much time on her make-up and had that smooth disdain characteristic of petty officials. In the compartments, glimpsed through the half-drawn limp little curtains, hedged in by babies, bags and bundles, men in shirt sleeves set out food on tables.

Here also Lenin presides, but I found him a much more human figure than the basilisk in the Leningrad Station. In the Kazan he is a little, brown, rather emaciated figure who greets you as you enter, looking not unlike Gandhi – seen from behind. I became fascinated by the various busts of Lenin. Lenin in his Asiatic mood; Lenin as the kindly uncle in the orphanage; Lenin as the wise counsellor, thoughtful and reflective in the old-age home; Lenin rough-hewn, craggy, kindly; Lenin with his hand in his pocket; Lenin leading the forces of the Revolution; Lenin in some statues with his right arm flung out before him, looking as if he has just thrown a frisbee.

'Leaving, I suppose, is a form of reading,' Valentin said.

He had a point. Certainly, leaving on an internal journey, from what I had heard of conditions for most Russian travellers, was more satisfying than arriving. And reading, like leaving, is one of the few private affairs permitted; it is the journey away from the place in which you find yourself, a secret route the State cannot follow. For however public the activity, the transports that readers and travellers enjoy, or endure, are private. Others may oversee them but their destinations remain unknown, like the motives which inspire their journeys. For this reason travellers become keenly aware of their solitude, even in crowds; it turns them inward, anxious to preserve themselves against official scrutiny. They become jealous of their space, possessive about their seats, careful of their privacy – in a word they are preoccupied, and the preoccupation of travellers, and readers, self-absorbed, remote, solitary, silent, is an extraordinary thing. Hundreds and hundreds of waiting travellers, utterly silent in railway stations, and bus stops, and airports, is one of the sights of Moscow. A reader in a park or on a bus reveals the same steady absorption. The stress and anxiety arises, I think, because although the reasons for travelling, like the reasons for reading, are personal, and even secret, yet the whole thrust of this society demands that everything be public, communal, and this redoubles the tension that exists between individuals and officials, the givers of permission.

There is nothing like doing it yourself, so a couple of times I left on internal journeys and found the fun was all in the departure, never in what followed, moments of terror, or boredom or anger. There are four local airports in Moscow and any one will do for those wishing to replicate my experience.

The destination, remember, is not important. What passengers require is transport. What the staff require is obedience. Travel is cheap, popular, disorganised and uncomfortable. These contradictory elements give flying its unique quality. Passengers arrive with straining bundles and plump string bags, boxes of all types and materials, and they wait. The shortages endemic elsewhere are also found at the airport. Planes often wait for an incoming flight with a little fuel left over in its tanks so they can top up. When the call comes to board, it should be treated with caution. Foreign touring parties take precedence. Big black limos sail out across the tarmac to deposit itinerant big-shots. An impressive delay while the crew march out, pilots in hats crazed with gold braid and as big as frying pans. Into what space remains, when all the important ones are in place, the passengers must dispose themselves and their goods as best they can. Oranges, bottles of beer, parcels of flowers, radio sets and bags of potatoes may be stuffed and sculpted into the open, overhead luggage racks. Thus into what little legal space there is, anything may go, at least in theory. Nothing is forbidden, everything is possible. *And vice versa.* The hostesses look on with weary disdain; airborne psychiatric nurses, the sight of the passengers tires and distresses them, they have sensitive nerves, and so they vanish. Optional seat belts, broken seats, invisible crew. Foreign passengers repeat, 'Soviet pilots orbit the earth!' Then, with the plane bursting at the seams, hear the metallic squeal of a key turning in the tail door, confirming that all have been locked in for the duration. Who knows how many have fallen victim to sudden turbulence in flight, some hapless Georgian or homebound Armenian felled by a flying ham or a pair of snow boots. At some point the hostesses reappear from their hiding places and offer fruit cordial and little souvenirs of the 1980 Moscow Olympics, and plastic racing cars.

Once, in the spring, I took the overnight train to Orel, about five hundred kilometres south of Moscow, a town rich in the remains of celebrated writers: vivid traces remain of Leskov and Bunin, Fet and Turgenev. As my train pulled out of the station, a boy ran down the platform holding the hand of his departing girl, until the speed of the train left him standing, hands on his hips, bending double from the waist, gasping for breath and unable to wave, bowing like a courtier after a departing princess. The velvet May evening pressed in solicitously, a smooth warm pressure, like plush in a jeweller's box. Spring nights in Moscow seemed at once priceless and oppressive.

From her little room at the end of the carriage the floor lady, stocky, stern and official arose like a djinn, offering tea from the samovar and warning against smoking in the compartments. With a special key produced from her bosom she opened a window in the passageway outside the compartments just a crack, hardly enough to get the air circulating, and even then this only made the evening more heavily oppressive by hinting at the way things might have been if she'd done the decent thing and opened the windows wide and let the wind blow. I was new and understood nothing. I asked her to open another window. She simply walked back to her little room, sat down and grew dark red until she glowed like a bar heater. 'No,' she would not open the window, 'No,' she would not leave her seat again and, certainly, 'No,' she would not even allow me to glimpse the key, *her* key, the sacred means by which this carriage, our world, might, or might not, be transformed. She constantly touched the key, hidden in her breast, as if to check that it was still there, in case I'd worked some magic and stolen it away. I knew that feeling, when everything depended on some small but essential piece of equipment: a passport, a wallet, knife, ring, vial, a rabbit's foot, pacemaker, arch support, and its proud but anxious owner tended to tap the vital object as if sending a message of reassurance to his inner self. She looked cornered. I stayed where I was, feeling that if I advanced on her she would panic and quite possibly swallow the key.

She was the perfect embodiment of what Hamlet called 'the insolence of office', that preening, armoured, petty pride; she showed it like some high decoration, she wore it like a medal. And medals are to the point; Muscovites are fond of giving medals – they are second only to the Americans in this regard. I think that this explains their love of badges. Badges, after all, are just medals you can buy – and wear without permission. What would Hamlet have called this country and its strange capital? I think he would have called it home. I thought of those duplicitous signs sometimes displayed in English liquor shops or sub-post offices: *Please do not ask for credit as a refusal may offend.* They are often headed: *Polite Notice.* In Moscow it is not the refusal, but the request, which offends. The naive, logical foreigner learns painfully that 'polite notices' are made up of mere words, words, words, of empty signs, and the giving of offence goes without saying. Looking at the key lady tapping her left breast on that warm evening in May I knew I would have to throw away my maps and read Hamlet.

I asked her again. This time the djinn, tea lady, key lady, simply left her seat, without changing colour now, or even frowning. I think she may even have smiled a little. At any rate she came down the corridor towards me and reached inside her dress for the key. I felt that sudden rush of relief and embarrassment we feel when an expected obstacle gives way suddenly, when anticipated unpleasantness fails to materialise. She was going to do what I asked. Then, in one expert, practised movement, she closed the window and locked it.

By the time I had got over my shock I wanted to applaud. Her move had finesse, economy, finality. Unbeknown to me we had been playing a silent game of chess, I had threatened her king and she had just mated me. If she had not been a key lady, she would have been a grand master. And her name was Legion, she was one of a gigantic sisterhood who occupied the seats of power all over the Soviet Union. In that carriage she was queen and against her edicts there was no appeal. You breathed a little, by her dispensation, or you suffocated.

3

My Cousin Hamlet

I met Hamlet in a Moscow flat and, as expected, he wore black and spoke well. But he preached sedition. He was one of those 'anti-socialist elements' the authorities rail against; it was hardly surprising that the king of the country wanted him locked up and had already locked up others who made similar speeches. His eyes were dark and bloodshot and he looked as if he had seen a ghost.

Unexpectedly, Hamlet turned out to be an Armenian. He was accompanied by an entourage, who somehow kept him going, men who were plumper than he was and ministered to him with affection and pride. They were also better dressed than Hamlet and rather jolly. They reminded me of handlers with a good boxer; they were proud of their boy and believed he could not lose. Hamlet was tired, there were shadows beneath his blazing eyes, he was gaunt, he looked as thin as my finger, but he felt a mile high, you could see that. And his back-up crew, healthy though they were, paled by comparison; after all they were merely human while Hamlet was full of turbulent and dangerous lunacies. What I could not work out, at least not at first, was why he seemed familiar.

We met in a church, though it would not have been recognised as one by any but the initiated (and those who, presumably, watch and report on them). The gathering was not secret, but it was private, an assembly of believers in an upstairs room, and sometimes the Pentecostal spirit was there, in the tongues of flame rising shakily from the candles which each person held, shielding them against the evening breeze which blew through the windows and rattled the picture of Mother Teresa on the wall.

Since the authorities disabled the Orthodox Church and banned all others after the Revolution, people have gone to church elsewhere. They have founded their own, set up secret chapels in unexpected venues from the wine-shop to the circus, or in the spaces within themselves. Alternative, ingenious, sometimes eccentric arrangements have been made for spiritual expression and celebration ever since the days when churches were dynamited, or closed, or became printing works, potteries or offices, their towers and bells lopped (the official mark of State castration). Passionate congregations assemble in unlikely places of worship; and worship may look like something else.

I was taken to meet Hamlet and an association of like-minded 'friends' by Nadia, dark-haired, vibrant, restless, a woman fired by the possibilities for change promised in the thousands of words spoken about perestroika, yet fearful that this spring, like so many others, would abruptly freeze over. 'And it is our last chance. Our very last chance!' Electrified by her sense of things to be done, yet appalled by the paralysis of her friends and colleagues who seemed to her to be choked in concrete and unwilling to bestir themselves, Nadia burnt with a fever many found disconcerting. Among her colleagues, her enthusiasm seemed rather onerous because it was at heart accusatory. Even her friends and family sensed her unspoken reproach. Yet her courage was extraordinary. She was afraid of nothing, not even of appearing silly. Only sometimes her faith and hope faltered – and when it did it was shocking to observe that what lay behind them was black despair.

The apartment block, in one of the oldest quarters of Moscow, was shabby. The grimy, pungent foyer had been used as a walk-in urinal, and the rickety wooden lift with its heavy steel door (all Moscow lifts are built to the same design) groaned on its cables as we climbed to a dishevelled but comfortable apartment on the sixth floor. On one wall was a portrait of Mother Teresa; pushed against the wall, flanked by an old piano and a large TV set, a small table was laid with a cloth on which there swam fierce black fish. On the table stood a slim blue candle and a small, newly baked loaf of bread. The congregation was ecumenical: Russian Orthodox priests, lay people, Armenian Nationalist Christians, and Seventh-Day Adventists. All held candles and all were encouraged to speak. Most people offered prayers for peace and reconciliation.

And then it was Hamlet's turn. Maybe no one had read him the rules. Maybe he knew them and did not care. He was just back from the Armenian enclave of Nagorno-Karabakh which lay on the other side of the Caucasus, a war zone with an Armenian Christian majority held in hated subjugation by the Moslem Republic of Azerbaijan. For the first time in living memory Moslems and Christians had clashed violently on the streets of previously unheard-of towns, like Stepanakert. Russian troops had been dispatched to stop the killing, but despite their presence it had continued for days. Excited reports reaching Moscow spoke of the flag of the Iranian revolution flying in Baku, capital of Moslem Azerbaijan. Young Russian soldiers trying to separate the warring parties were sliced to pieces. The combatants reviled them, wished them gone, drove trucks into them. Boys from Siberian villages began arriving home in coffins. The Armenian citizens of Nagorno-Karabakh demanded that the enclave be reunited with the Armenian motherland. Azerbaijanis rioted in Baku when they learnt of the demand. Moscow refused. It imposed direct rule and it ordered the arrest of the committee which led the demands. Armenian and Moslem refugees fled the enclave in their hundreds and headed for the safety of their religious strongholds. Hamlet had watched these events unfold and, with the agony of the Armenian earthquake still fresh in his mind, he had decided to go on the road and preach the gospel of Armenian unity, sanctity and spiritual destiny.

'The freedom struggle in Armenia', he announced without apology in that apartment on the sixth floor in the centre of Moscow, 'is a struggle to recognise the will of God.'

The remainder of his passionate, eloquent but confusing sermon offered variations on this thesis. In Hamlet's vision the Armenians became a chosen people who could confer blessings on others, or withhold them, their destiny was special, favoured, guided from above. This is when I realised why his words had a familiar ring to them. I had heard these phrases before and I knew what they were, a rhetorical device particularly apt for tracing the powerful and menacing movement towards grace and favour for a special people – and punishment for those who do not hear the word. Nationalism and religion are indistinguishable; one can put forward a political programme which is underwritten by the Deity. I had heard it often from the mouths of the white Afrikaner nationalists of Southern Africa. I had heard it from black nationalists in Soweto. They had preached this way for decades and it had meant just one thing: trouble.

'The recognition of the will of God leaves people free in their hearts,' Hamlet promised. 'Freer than they are in Moscow. The struggle for freedom in Armenia is a message to the people of the Soviet Union: if we want to change the system, we must change ourselves first.' Hamlet's eyes were black as coals. He trembled with emotion and fatigue. From the wall Mother Teresa directed a calm glance at him. We stared at our candles and concentrated on keeping the blue wax from dripping on our hands. The feeling was that, yes, people were free, in that room that night, to speak as they chose, and certainly there was a sympathetic response to Hamlet's speech, but no one, I think, was prepared for this fighting talk. I felt then that if Hamlet's furious faith and raging sense of divine mission in Armenia's special destiny are shared by others in Armenia and in Nagorno-Karabakh since the Moslem pogroms, there are stormy times ahead and the Soviet government will have to arrest not just the nationalist committee but the entire Armenian nation before they can hope to contain it.

The rhetoric of special destinies, so adept at inflaming expectation, often ends badly. But at this moment it is a fire burning through the ethnic minorities in distant and, until recently, disregarded republics. Russia, which a few years ago announced it had 'solved the problems of Nationalities', did so in a way we recognise in South Africa: declare your distant ethnic homelands independent and then starve them of resources and govern them from the distant capital. In the heat of spreading nationalism it is difficult to see how the large republics, like Georgia and the Ukraine, will escape scorching.

In Hamlet this nationalism was to be heard in its purest and, to me, most familiar form.

Though it depressed me, I was also vaguely comforted simply by feeling rather sadly at home. Nationalism has been an unmitigated disaster for Africa where it has become merely the acceptable face of tribalism, and it was dispiriting to find on another continent the belief that tribalism was the future. For this was really behind Hamlet's rhetoric: tribal hatred, directed only partly against Moslems. His obvious (major) target was the government of the USSR, but that is largely composed of faceless, anonymous committee men, who serve as a cover for his real targets: the dominant majority, the Russians. Through the Russian empire the tribes are growing restless and the hot winds of change are blowing as they did once in Africa.

'God favours the Russian people,' Hamlet declared. (But he did not make it sound like a favour.) 'He wishes to bless them!' From the very tone and timbre of his voice it was clear that the Russians could expect the blessing to be deferred until such time as God – or Hamlet, since they were as one in the matter – decided to bestow it.

Afterwards Hamlet and I talked, surrounded by eager Russian listeners, while his attendants sipped tea and ate cake. Close up, Hamlet was even more drawn and tense than I had realised. Was his a political faith? I asked. His socks beneath his vintage black trousers were threadbare and hung about his ankles which he massaged gently as we sat in the bedroom.

Not at all, he insisted. The political struggle in Armenia was inseparable from a deep faith in the will of God.

But was it not fair to say that the Soviet Government was coming round, however slowly, to recognising that a measure of autonomy in the Transcaucasian republics of Armenia and Azerbaijan, and in the Baltic states of Estonia, Latvia and Lithuania was overdue?

Again he disagreed fiercely. To say this suggested that the Russians had something to offer the republics struggling for independence. The contrary was true. 'Merely by their struggle, the Baltic republics did more for freedom in Russia than the Russians can ever do for them. They point the way ahead. Surely Russians also wish to be free?'

'And what of Armenia? How do the authorities behave there?'
The black eyes burn. 'They have fallen back on the bad old ways. They take the Stalinist line.'

From that low point there was no way back to reasonable discussion. No insult could have wounded his listeners more deeply. No compromise seemed possible. His handlers moved in and began getting their boy together for the next round. He was going on to speak somewhere else that night.

Were there, I wondered as we parted, any Ophelias in Armenia?

He paused at the lift, encircled by his entourage. 'As far as I know, there are no Ophelias. But we have many Hamlets.'

Valentin has a friend in Azerbaijan. She is a Jew and he worries about her as reports of more killings come in daily. 'Suddenly the papers are full of places I've never heard of – Nakichevan and Kirobabad. Violent poetry!' His friend's difficulty is a special one. As a young girl, when anti-Semitism was popular among Armenian Christians, she adopted a Christian name. Now she wishes she had kept her original Jewish name: the Moslems are killing Christians – this time around Jews are not on the list. Valentin fetched up one of his icicle smiles from the deep freeze. 'Do you suppose this is progress?'

From the strange church in the sixth-floor apartment to what passes for the real thing is another way of reading Moscow, city of ruined churches. Only a rival religion which harboured an unspeakable fear of the spirit that built the great Moscow churches could have wreaked such malicious destruction upon them. But, as I discovered, that spirit was not exterminated: it changed its shape and went elsewhere. There were once, the old saying goes, 'forty times forty churches' in Moscow. More exact estimates suggest around four hundred and fifty churches. Stalin, the former theology student, demolished many; the Metro builders aided the destruction; time and woodworm accounted for still more; by the early 1940s Stalin had destroyed over ninety per cent of the churches; Krushchev was a zealous accomplice; and, later still, the Moscow planners of the sixties and seventies laid waste with a will. Churches were converted into factories, offices, art galleries and museums, with the result that today no more than six dozen working churches survive. In the changing political climate, some are being returned to their original owners and restored to their former use; but of late, conservation has brought new problems as some of those churches saved from ruin struggle to find new owners and occupations.

The modest museum of the history of Moscow occupies the neo-classical church of St John the Evangelist, a pretty pink building erected in 1825. An added bonus for the visitor is that it is opposite the KGB headquarters on Dzerzhinsky Square, though it will not be widely known that the area around the grim yet somehow prim KGB buildings was once richly crowded with churches. A blind fortress – among its many ghosts the insurance agents it once housed. Real change, for which so many hope, will only have come when Intourist begin running open-days at the Lubyanka jail and tours of the cellars where 'enemies of the people' were customarily shot by Stalin's police, and postcards go on sale at the door. At present there is a great debate on the form of a memorial to the victims of Stalin's camps and prisons. When we drove past KGB headquarters an acquaintance offered a typically Muscovite view.

'Why build a memorial for the victims? While Dzerzhinsky Square remains we already have the best monument available!'

The remark took on a flavour one might call 'Moscow piquant', coming from a man said by some to be a KGB operative.

With signal lack of evangelical fervour the museum exhibits, in the former crypt, prehistoric remains of Moscow and medieval models of the Kremlin. Also in the crypt is a hologram of Ivan the Terrible, and if you can persuade the attendant to turn on the light you may view the head of the tyrant in three dimensions, a golden, hawk-like, savage face. But what of the head of that other great monster who was so fascinated by him, the pock-marked, sallow Georgian with the bristly moustache? Surely it would be appropriate if Stalin were to be mounted beside Ivan the Terrible? The thought is tempting, political exposure and castigation of the old criminal are all very well, however difficulties would arise if fanatics started treating the head as a cult object. There are those who still remember him with great affection; good old Joe, they say, he kept prices down, queues short and goods in the shops, and if people suffered, well, they were the big-shots, weren't they? and so they deserved to suffer. He was the people's friend, the great leader, the one whom the poet Osip Mandelstam called the 'Kremlin mountaineer' – and died for it.

'. . . We all wore fur coats, silk stockings and patent-leather shoes . . . Joseph Stalin gave his all to the common people.' So wrote an admirer to a Moscow paper, enraged by recent attacks on the old leader. She speaks for many, though their views are out of fashion.

Images of Moscow are hard to fix and sometimes even harder to fathom – maybe because its beholders have wanted to shape the city in their likeness. In the eighteenth and nineteeth centuries, French painters got to work on Moscow and made it look rather like an Asiatic Vatican, or a Russian Versailles, dark green, well-watered, softly sandy and astonishingly lush. A century later, just before the Revolution, it was painted to seem modern, more brightly lit than it ever seems possible: a bridge over a river and a sunsplashed street, some bright corner of Paris perhaps? – were it not for the outrageous technicolored nodules of St Basil's Cathedral visible in the background. 'Blow up that mosque!' Napoleon snapped, before fleeing Moscow in 1812. But the Muscovites set fire to their city rather than allow it to remain in French hands – and his soldiers had more pressing concerns.

Photographs of Moscow a hundred years ago are eerie relics, scraps of dreams, showing a city steadily drawing towards the Western model: on the busy sidewalks butchers' boys, shop girls, spivs and cabbies, advertised by their collars, clothes, their hairstyles, hats and canes, that they belonged to a metropolitan culture linking the great capitals of Europe. Red Square was painted by visiting foreigners to look like the old Les Halles in Paris or Covent Garden in London, or Potsdamer platz in Berlin, a public meeting-ground, lively with hawkers, fruit stalls and a blossoming flower market, and one is grateful for this record of a colourful, pulsating street life. Sellers of fruit juice and *kvass* (fermented rye, fruit and sugar) set up their flagons upon rickety tables on the cobbles and poured generous glasses in much the same way as their descendants do today in the kiosks of the Yaroslavl railway station. All that vivid various energy has long departed: the knife-grinder at his wheel, the itinerant cobbler who worked on the spot, the chicken sellers with their great boat-shaped basket of live birds, carried on their heads like enormous wicker-work panama hats – all gone, and with them a lightness, a love of colour and movement at which many of the paintings and the photographs hint, the bustling vivacity of street life in 'old Moscow'. In the Moscow Museum today, somnolent floor ladies rouse themselves, their dry coughs warning you not to linger before the glass cases of pretty fossils from another time and place: school reports confirming excellence in Greek; ivory opera glasses; silly hats.

The museum is there to conceal as much as it preserves of the city, past and present, but there are rewards and perhaps even intimations of things to come. The sharp-eyed will find on the second floor a forlorn black-and-white photograph of the former Moscow Stock Exchange. Little rooms at the very top of the house are said to contain, as it were, 'Moscow of the future' presented in drawings and sketches. Sadly, as with so much else in the heady talk of progress, it seems that passage into more modern times may be arbitrarily restricted. When I tried to visit the upper rooms the attendants barred my way; no one was being allowed up the stairs.

'Do you think the future is being refurbished?' Valentin murmured as we left the museum and the floor ladies gratefully doused the lights, returned to their seats and went back to sleep.

For good or ill, the Kremlin draws all Moscow towards it. Paradoxically, although it is built on a small hill, everything seems to flow *down* into the Kremlin. It is, I suppose, the weight of the place, the dead centre of the city. I went often to the Kremlin, unable to resist its fatal attractions: seventy acres of towers, battlements, walls, churches, palaces, domes, steeples, red stars, a fortress (for that is what a *kreml* is) in the shape of a rough triangle on the Moskva River, presiding over the cobbled parade ground and aching spaces of Red Square. Though the Kremlin is widely advertised as the place to go in Moscow, most of it remains off-limits, locked, forbidding and secretive as ever it was under the Tsars. Shortly after the Revolution it was closed to all but the rulers. And it remained shut until 1956, a more severe quarantine than anything imposed by the Tsars.

Views of the Kremlin have varied over the years, the impressions of the traveller changing in the light of his nationality and political beliefs in much the way that the ice-cream and pineapple domes of St Basil's Cathedral may appear poisonous or delectable according to the season and time of day and the mood of the observer. The Marquis de Custine noted in the mid-eighteenth century that the Kremlin belonged to a man who possessed absolute power, that absolute power was always monstrous and the monster had built itself a house in Moscow. The Kremlin, de Custine suggested, was really just a collection of dungeons which its power-mad owner considered churches and palaces. You did not *live* in the Kremlin, he muttered darkly, you holed up in it. The Tsar might deny it but architecture spoke more loudly than denials. The Russians, de Custine suggested in a prophetic moment, anticipating the anguished cry of the poet Alexander Blok, seemed doomed to imprison themselves, try as they might to escape.

However, the Marquis's Gallic disdain does not fully cover the question, for on many occasions the Kremlin needed its stout defences. From the earliest times when the Russians rose in ascendancy over the Tartars in 1380, and government and Church were consolidated in this great fortress on the Moskva River, it has been attacked by Moslems, Swedes, Poles, Lithuanians, Frenchmen and the Tsars' own mutinous subjects. When Lenin closed 'the window on the West', which Peter the Great had opened in St Petersburg, and returned to Moscow to set up the new Revolutionary government in 1918, he was doing something Russian rulers had done for centuries: withdrawing into the fortress of the Kremlin, an impulse which went back to the beginnings of the city when Prince Dolgoruky, founder of Moscow, surrounded Kremlin Hill with a wooden fence in the middle of the twelfth century.

De Custine's trenchant observations are more than matched by views of Muscovites themselves who, moreover, possess a delicate sense of the ridiculous which enables them to register more sharply than any visitor the contradictory treasures of the Kremlin. In the nineteenth century, the writer Chaadayev was already pointing to the absurdities to be found in the city by earnest tourists. Moscow was an amazing place, said Chaadayev, full of objects notable for being ridiculous, like the eighteenth-century Tsar's Bell, and the Great Cannon, made in the sixteenth century. The bell, which is over six metres high and weighs over two hundred tonnes, is the largest in the world. But it cracked soon after casting and has never been heard. The great forty-tonne cannon dates from 1586 and is also the world's largest. It was the brainchild of Ivan the Terrible's son. Not surprisingly, perhaps, Tsar Fyodor Ivanovich preferred peace to war, and the gun has never been fired. The tradition continues. Visitors to the Kremlin are invited to admire the functional 'modern' Palace of Congresses. Built in an enormous hurry by Nikita Krushchev in the early sixties, it is all glass and steel and its bland modernity contrasts strangely with the brutal splendour of the Kremlin's palaces and churches. It is as if one had come across a Cossack carrying a briefcase.

Of all the Kremlin's treasures, its churches are the most beautiful and have the additional advantage of being open to all. This is due to the fact that they are churches no longer, but State museums with admission by ticket, painted shells of their former selves, holy ghosts. The palaces and treasure houses of the Kremlin often require the visitor to gain permission for a visit, or to attend with a group, and the merciless onward surge of these ensembles destroys the single useful purpose of going into such places at all: the luxury of being allowed to ponder and absorb at leisure. Frantic groups of East Germans and Britons are lashed on by the impatient cheerleaders waving red handkerchiefs who hurry them through the painted Hall of Facets in order to race through the treasures of the Armoury. Official touristic practice in the Soviet Union holds that the visitors' progress should be hasty and uncomfortable, perhaps in the hope that they will not make the mistake again.

But in the churches freedom reigns. Once past the watchful door ladies (the ecclesiastical equivalent of hotel floor ladies) you may linger. Winter visits are best. There are few foreign tourists and Soviet visitors predominate, shoals of young pioneers in red scarves, and visiting Siberians who ebb and flow about the painted columns staring up at the great iconostasis, the giant altar screen where the icons hang, showing on their faces bewilderment tinged with awe at finding themselves among the ruins of some glorious but extinguished foreign civilisation. Troubled Soviet eyes stare up at the icons and the saints stare serenely back.

My favourite is the Uspensky Cathedral, also known as the Cathedral of the Dormition. I was accompanied sometimes by Ivan, a poet from the provinces. Ivan was a hunchback and a dwarf and a born storyteller. He regretted the changed times because, he told me, in the olden days he could have made a living as a travelling storyteller.

'All the Tsars had them, it was traditional. Ivan the Terrible couldn't go to sleep at night until his storytellers had soothed him with stories to dream by.'

The Cathedral of the Dormition contained the great wooden throne of Ivan the Terrible, carved with scenes depicting the transference of Christian spiritual power from the Byzantine Emperor Constantine to Prince Vladimir of Kiev after the fall of Constantinople in 1453. Ivan the hunchback loved to linger there.

'Because of this divine succession, Moscow called itself the third Rome,' Ivan explained, staring up at his namesake's throne. 'It's part of my heritage, Moscow, the third Rome. Why should I be deprived of it? I could have been a royal storyteller, perhaps. Now I am not even a member of the writers' union.'

There have been other names for Moscow. The nineteenth-century writer and revolutionary Alexander Herzen, homesick in English exile long before the Revolution, called it 'the people's capital'. Lord Curzon thought it more like a 'Christian Cairo', and recently it has been described by an American president as the capital of the evil empire. Moscow adapts itself to many definitions and conforms to none.

Ivan did not come to the Kremlin churches in order to admire their beauty. 'I want to remind myself of those who burnt the forests of our faith, and those who died defending them.' He pointed to the golden summerhouse of a tomb which contains the remains of a seventeenth-century patriarch, imprisoned by the Poles after they invaded Moscow in 1612 and left to starve to death. When visiting children grew bored, Ivan would tell them stories about the Tsar's great chair and the patriarch's tomb. Tourists, prevented by the door ladies from taking photographs of the church, took photographs of Ivan instead, and the door ladies did not object. Indeed, the looks in their eyes and those of the children when Ivan appeared were close to the visionary gleam in the eyes of Gennady, the demented cab driver, when the pigeon descended to his car in Kalinin Prospekt and ancient memories of the Holy Ghost stirred in his heart.

'All Russians adore a good story.' Ivan loved to quote Gogol's remark, from his story *The Overcoat*. But the looks in the eyes of his audience sometimes made me wonder if there was not another ancient predilection at work among Muscovites when they contemplated his stunted body. For not only did the Tsars delight in stories, but also they kept dwarfs, negroes, apes and parrots for their diversion. In the seventeenth century the Tsar Mikhail owned sixteen dwarfs, and Peter the Great kept half a dozen to play with when he was a child. Dwarfs and fools were housed separately in the Royal Court; the dwarfs for some reason were in charge of the royal parrots. The Russian sightseers stared at Ivan as if trying to remember something. Ivan did not care. He was quite proud of his disability and the attention flattered him.

'There are those who compare Ivan the Terrible and Stalin. Ask me which was worse? Well, just think: Ivan loved his storytellers. Stalin murdered his!'

The foundation stone of the Cathedral of the Dormition (dedicated to the departed spirit of the Virgin) was laid in 1326 to celebrate the deliverance of Moscow from the Tartars, though there had probably been a church on the site well before that date. This marks the period from which Moscow dates as the capital of the Russian State, ruled by the Muscovite princes who traced their ancestry back to the Emperor Augustus and hence laid claim to the title 'Tsar'. A new cathedral was built in 1472 on the instructions of the Grand Prince Ivan the Third, who was also responsible for rebuilding the Kremlin. The architects were two Russians, Krivtsov and Myshkin. Unfortunately, soon after the new cathedral was opened on May 20th, 1474, it fell down. One hesitates to imagine the fate of Krivtsov and Myshkin. As a result of this disaster an Italian architect called Fioravante planned the present building, which dates from 1479. A contemporary chronicler delighted in its 'light, sonority and space'. He spoke truly. Even crowded with tourists it seems somehow to contain them all without difficulty and to soar above them. Five domes, blind arches, and white stone perspective portals, four great circular pillars holding up the roof, painted all the way from floor to ceiling; upon the towering iconostasis apostles, Christs and angels soar heavenward. In particular there is an olive-skinned Christ with blood-red petal lips. His broad gold halo is flaking but it is the rosy flesh of the lips glowing in the dark face that take the eye: they seem almost to be pursed for a kiss. His dark forked beard and darker ringlets open like the estuaries of small rivers, and the golden disc encircling the face flows into the hair. It is a sensuous, haunting face, far more disconcerting than the famous and very beautiful fourteenth-century Byzantine icon of Christ near by, known as 'the Christ of the Severe Eye' – a face more animated, less visionary, the forehead lined, black eyes not 'severe' but piercing, a look of fine intelligence and confidence.

Also close by is a copy of the famous Virgin of Vladimir, a painting called 'Our Lady of Perpetual Succour', a Madonna and Child – well, not so much a child as a child-man, rendered in the Byzantine manner, as if the child were really a little adult, a midget. He sits there, the child-man, on the seat of his mother's hand, which is curved like a saddle or the branch of a tree beneath his neat posterior, and kisses her cheek. She wears red with a fringe of green showing beneath her mantle. The tourists seldom look up. It is probably just as well, for, painted in the domes high above their heads, huge dark-eyed Christs stare fiercely down at the Lilliputian Soviet citizens far below.

Near by, the Cathedral of the Archangel Michael has the air of a royal waiting room, dusty, long shuttered, the attendants confused about just what they are doing there. This was the communal burial place of the Russian kings: Tsars, princes and military leaders going back to the fourteenth century lie in bronze-encased tombs which look like large suitcases stacked one next to the other against the walls; the abandoned luggage of departed giants.

Fascinating for unexpected reasons is the fifteenth-century Cathedral of the Annunciation which, like the other once-sacred places in the Kremlin, says something not about religion but about the way things are in contemporary Russia; says it by way of three of its icons situated to the left of the sacred doors leading through the iconostasis to the altar. The icons portray, side by side, a very beautiful Madonna, the Archangel Gabriel and the figure of Christ. The Madonna is anxious, a little tense, sad and remote. Dressed in gold, the child sits in her lap and appears to be giving her soothing counsel. He is bald, or at least shaved, right down to a jet of nut-brown hair which is worn in a kind of punk or mohawk style, contrasting strangely with the Buddha-like impassivity of the old-young face. But look closely and you will see a large piece of sticking tape on the Virgin's right arm, as if she has sustained a wound there. Once you start noticing such things you cannot stop: a strip of sticking tape on the Madonna and Child; several more on the Christ figure – and they are all over the Archangel Gabriel: frail beauty held together with Sellotape.

Many of the icons to be seen in the former churches of the Kremlin are not genuine; they are copies of originals which were collected in art galleries after the Revolution. Despite the apparent iconoclasm of the Bolsheviks, Russians remained passionate iconophiles; the triumph of Stalinism served merely to ensure that secular icons of political leaders increasingly replaced the images of the saints. And this was hardly new. The replacement of one set of icons by another, reflecting the supersession of one set of beliefs by a competing system, is as old as the Eastern Church, where there has long been a tradition of these wars fought with pictures, going back to the great iconoclast crisis in eighth-century Byzantium. Into the vacuum left in the spiritual consciousness after the destruction and suppression of religious icons following the Revolution, there flowed countless portraits of Lenin, Stalin and Brezhnev; holy, even miraculous, images of the sanctified ones, venerated by their followers, buttressed by their slogans and claiming the right of divine succession. 'Stalin is Lenin today!' the schoolchildren of the thirties were taught to proclaim, and Brezhnev's jauntier claim to kinship with the founding father neatly leapfrogged the disgraced Stalin by asserting: 'From Illych to Illych!' The rich confusion between sacred and secular images in the minds of many may be observed still. The crowds of Soviet visitors who stare with incomprehension or mounting embarrassment at saints and divinities painted in an orgy of reverence in the Uspensky Cathedral, think nothing of laying flowers before a bust of Lenin. A little girl, daughter of an Orthodox believer, turns perplexed to her mother: 'But we never put flowers in front of *our* icons.'

The exploitation of certain icons over others in order to direct the faith of the people continues an ancient Byzantine tradition. No Christ or Virgin or saint in the Church calendar can have given rise to such an army of icons as Joseph Stalin, once sincerely believed by millions to be the heroic and perfect embodiment of man on earth. Yet the Kremlin, once a temple crowded with his images and sacred to his cult, no longer knows him. Where are they now? In some vault the countless icons wait for the new museums where they will surely be displayed one day to be wondered over by visitors with the same puzzlement and anxiety with which many of them may be seen staring up at the Christ of the Severe Eye.

I began to see that church-going was undertaken for all the wrong reasons. Wrong reasons are the staple in Moscow for doing most things. A confusion of tourists, an indifference of officials, a divine service of ignorance – that is what most church-going entails. The young soldiers at the service, *homo sovieticus*, eyes wide with disbelief at the priests in their golden crowns; tourists with camera transplants where their eyes once were. At the Novodovichy Convent the painters always busy outside the wall, painting over and over again, small watercolours of the convent's walls, bell towers, floating domes. This is the way to do it, over and over, as if one day you might get things right. You see artists doing the same thing before St Basil's, as if after all these years they cannot quite believe their eyes.

In Moscow words frequently fail, perhaps because they have failed so many so often; the currency is almost valueless. Reality lies in the spots or blemishes, in what is left out of the picture, never in the broad strokes, in the confident modelling that conventionally makes for representation. Truth lies almost, but not quite, in looking away, in the detail almost missed, the one that snags the imagination and makes it see.

It was to the Novodovichy Convent, in the seventeenth century, that Peter the Great exiled his sister Sophia and forced her to take the veil, after an abortive revolt against him. Among the Tsars of the seventeenth and eighteenth centuries, the Hamletic urge to punish women branded as faithless by locking them in nunneries was strong. The Novodovichy Convent was the favoured place for confining ambitious women, the most dangerous nunnery in Moscow. Three of the men who had presented petitions to Sophia, and who were thus seen as the leaders of the conspiracy to overthrow the Tsar, were hanged outside her window with the same petitions clutched in their hands. So close to her window were the dangling men that she could reach out and touch them.

According to Ivan the poet, the best way of seeing Red Square was from toe level, facing St Basil's Cathedral with the Lenin Museum behind you.

'Down on your knees, lower your nose almost to the cobbles and then look up. This ensures the finest view. Also it makes sure that you assume the proper position of humility in this place of ghosts and heroes.'

I tried it, following Ivan who did it more fluently and attracted less attention, being closer to the ground to begin with. The effect of looking up almost as your nose touches the cobbles is that you see, or think you are seeing, the curvature of the earth.

As Ivan put it, 'Red Square, like the earth, isn't flat. Though many believe it is.'

'Look, Ma,' said a child, 'a mullah and his son!'

Red Square has been emptied of everything; only its size

remains to impress, and to deter. Two great avenues have been blasted clear on either side of the Lenin Museum, linking Red Square with the enormous, windswept wilderness of October Square, which was created by demolishing everything between the area bounded by what used to be called Mokhovaya Street and the Alexandrovsky Gardens. Such spaces were cleared to make room for tanks and marching men and the great mechanical displays dictators love. The size of these spaces, seen either from the cobbles or from the air, is overwhelming; there is something brutal about the scope of the intention, the crusading emptiness, the creation of policed deserts intended to destroy all sense of human scale. The remaking of Moscow by Stalin was an assault on the personal and, more lethally, on the *person* from whose hands the modest, intimate, manageable scales of measurement were torn, and in their place went the exaltation of the mass and the massive; that is his legacy to the city: architecture as war.

October Square is a commemorative void. Its emptiness recalls the cult of Stalin and his urge to lay waste on a grand scale; a portrait in stone and tarmac of Stalin's mind: 'Let there be nothing but me – and let the nothing be everywhere.' There is the Moskva Hotel built in 1935, bleak, huge, lopsided with its two mismatched wings. Legend has it that when the architects (who included Shchusev, designer of Lenin's Mausoleum) showed Stalin the drawing with different wings, intending that the Boss should choose the style he liked. Stalin misunderstood. 'Build it just like that,' he said. And of course they did. I have sat in the Moskva Hotel drinking Moskovskoe beer, Stalin's favourite, with an ancient veteran who liked to gatecrash my table and improve his English, 'Listen, I speak: one, three, nine . . .' while telling me stories about his wartime experiences. His battalion was raised in Minsk and fought its way into Berlin. Whenever the waiter objected to his villainous yellow cigarettes, the old man flashed his metal teeth and pointed to the noble salad of campaign ribbons on his chest and the waiter retreated. The old soldier remained devoted to Stalin, though he liked to claim he'd seen through him.

'Look, once we believed that without Stalin we would stop

living. Drop down dead, just like that! Well, Comrade Stalin has gone, but I'm still here!' The metal teeth glinted and he pulled contentedly at his beer.

In Red Square the air cleared and sharpened as the sun set and the temperature began dropping, the last of the daylight settling like luminous frost. The gigantic bronze figures in front of St Basil's, commemorating Russian resistance to the invading Poles of 1612, threw up their hands as if to ward off the darkening chill. A policeman slapped his grey coat with his truncheon; it made a dry, bleak sound. Each cobble in the immense square seemed to rise more rounded and obstinate under foot. An American girl in a group of passing tourists said aloud, 'I've looked for him and I simply can't find him, anywhere in the world.' In the car park behind St Basil's, and in the icy shadows of the Kremlin wall, the big black limousines of the delegates to the Supreme Soviet waited, endless rows of them drawn up to attention, engines ticking over. It was as if a multitude of witches had flown in for a high-level coven and had parked their broomsticks outside.

'The delegates are meeting to discuss further reforms to the electoral system,' Valentin explained. He had that glazed, vacant look which signalled his distaste for this charade. The way he spoke, the men inside the Kremlin might have been engaged in unspeakable practices with furry animals.

St Basil's in winter was always colder inside than out. The floor ladies and door ladies wore coats and hats all day and sat in front of little electric bar heaters; some burrowed so deeply into their furs they looked like hibernating squirrels. St Basil's Cathedral is disconcertingly bare indoors, but full of weapons. Downstairs were glass cases of the bows and arrows, the battle-axes, captured by Ivan the Terrible from the Khan of Kazan in the sixteenth century, a jagged treasure of chainmail, swords and scimitars. Behind wooden screens workmen continued the restoration of the interior which has been going on since St Basil's opened its doors again to visitors in 1978. Through a six-inch crack beneath the partition I glimpsed the restorers at work. They were sitting on the floor cementing bricks into place. A hand reached out, lifted a brick, examined it as if it were a loaf of bread or a piece of cheese, tapped it with a trowel, tapped it again, discarded it for reasons unknown and worked ceased for long minutes. Boredom and an air of bafflement leaked from beneath the partition – no one understood what tourists were doing there. They probably did not understand what *they* were doing there. Nobody understood anything – or if they did, they were not saying.

As darkness fell, Red Square emptied except for the police; even the never-ending line of sightseers queuing to see Lenin's tomb vanished. The militia men walked up and down swinging their truncheons and blowing their whistles. The whistling reached a crescendo when a convoy of big black limousines sped through the Kremlin gate carrying some important person home to dinner. The colours of St Basil's domes died suddenly, as if someone had switched them off.

St Basil's was built by Ivan the Terrible to commemorate his victory over the Tartars of Kazan in 1552. Today Kazan is raising its head again. Gangs of young people are coming up to Moscow from faraway Kazan, and mugging the general public. They lie in wait in subways and in the Metro stations and relieve victims of their jackets, of their shopping, of their cameras. The appearance of these gangs are known as 'guest performances'. Such is the fear aroused by the name 'Kazan' that the mere mention of it is enough to frighten owners of co-operatives into handing over protection money to the thugs that prey upon them. In a sense I suppose you could say that four hundred years after Ivan the Terrible put them down, the boys from Kazan are back in town.

An hour later the big limousines still waited with their engines turning. The world was divided into three classes, those with cars and drivers, those with cars, and those with neither. As we walked past a line of these black marias parked in a solid ring around St Basil's, sending their exhaust fumes up to heaven like poisonous prayers, I said to Valentin, 'This sort of thing makes breathing difficult. Better hold your breath.'

'I can't go on holding my breath forever,' said Valentin.

We skirted the Lobnoe Mesto elevation, a circular platform where royal edicts were read out and executions took place in front of St Basil's, and walked into that other temple on Red

Square where the faithful come to worship, the GUM department store with its arcades and swirling crowds. Three deep, they stood in silence before a small range of tape recorders, old-fashioned monsters with great whirring spools, and a small selection of more modern cassette players. Two young shop assistants lounged against the far end of the wooden counter, gazing at the machines as if at any moment they might burst into flames. A sign above the counter stated: *Colour Television Sets*. One of the cassette machines was playing rock music, clumsily pirated from a Western tape, a thick, wet, sandy music that sounded as if it were being forced through mud. No one spoke – what need was there for words? Words were useless, words said things like 'Colour Television Sets'. The two assistants had nothing to sell; the customers found nothing they wanted to buy. No one moved. Time turned to ice and we slowly froze over.

Behind St Basil's is the Moskvoretsky Bridge which leads to the old Zamoskvorechye quarter, across the Moskva River. It was the Moskvoretsky Bridge which so enchanted painters in the eighteenth and nineteenth and early twentieth centuries that they returned to it again and again. None of them would know the drab thoroughfare now were it not for the lickable domes of St Basil's in the background.

The Church of St Nicholas, a white and gold church in the Zamoskvorechye district, was built in 1681 and restored in the nineteenth century. One of the few churches to have preserved its treasures and its function through the years of blood and ice, it is still aromatic with the scents of the way that things were, candlewax, woollen coats, incense, head-scarves, felt boots and the papery prayers of devout old women who form the core of most congregations. Devotional lamps hanging before the framed icons have a secretive, oily, stubborn gleam. Some icons are clothed in silver, a nineteenth-century ornament, only their faces and fingers and little feet peep through, not guarded by the silver sheath. They reveal an ancient skin tan imparted by the smoke of thousands and thousands of pencil-thin tapers, endlessly replenished in the candle-stands before each sacred image. St

Nicholas's is a working church, a place of worship, and this is reflected by the settled confidence of the place, the beggars in the porch, the calm, unhurried prayers of the worshippers before the icons.

A little to one side of the nave, a stocky priest in blue vestments was giving counsel to a line of parishioners who queued patiently to speak to him. Their problems were many and each was dealt with in a gentle, courteous but highly professional way. A family had questions about burying their dead: how should it be done? What were the colours of the bindings to be? What was the ritual for the laying out of the body? Patiently the priest explained, sometimes resting his hand on the shoulder of the questioner and when a particularly technical point had to be made, he would cite chapter and verse from the books on the lectern in front of him. An old lady in felt boots, heavy coat and shawl tightly wrapped around her head approached him hesitantly. She wished, she confided, in a tremulous voice, to make a journey to Kiev where she had heard there was a holy man, a particular priest who would be able to renew her faith, put her in touch with God. The little round priest embraced her. A journey to Kiev was a serious undertaking. And she did not know who she was looking for. How would she find him when she arrived there?

'It doesn't matter. I must go, this holy man will bring me peace.'

'It's a long journey for an old person,' the priest replied. 'And it's not a good idea. Tell me, would you set off on a journey every time someone suggested it to you? Are you going to venture into the unknown every time somebody tells you that a holy man will put you in touch with God? Stay here, this church is good enough for you and me. Stay here and pray, God is no further away in Moscow than he is in Kiev, it is both as easy and as difficult to touch him here.'

The old lady blessed herself repeatedly and thanked him, kissing his hand. The priest was old and tired and unfailingly patient. He was spiritual adviser, psychiatrist, doctor, friend, legal adviser, and all his audiences were conducted in public. Those who wished to discuss very intimate matters would step close and whisper into his ear, around which he cupped his hand to amplify the whispered confidences.

[82]

The new order that came to power after 1918 despised such movements of the human heart and attacked the impulses that make them possible – call them charity, or kindness or imaginative sympathy – and so public dealings between Muscovites are notable for their crudeness, rudeness and insensitivity. Delicate, personal concern was rare, and costly. Someone who knew the priest asked me to guess his age. I put him in his early seventies. He was fifty-six.

Hamlet was intemperate; he wanted all or nothing, for him the choice was freedom, or slavery. He also wanted revenge. Blood. For our blood. In short, I recognised now why he too had seemed so familiar. Hamlet was very like Nationalist friends of mine, black and white, in South Africa. Hamlet was family. And maybe he showed the way ahead. He paid Gorbachev the compliment of taking him at his word. If perestroika was to mean more than mouthings, empty gestures, big talk in the Kremlin and empty mouths in the provinces, if perestroika was to be more than its achievement thus far – a revolution from above – then it would have to take root on the edges of society, in the country, in the provinces, in the disregarded republics and among the despised minorities. Because one thing was sure: the revolution was not taking place in Moscow. In Moscow the intellectuals were having a wordy holiday and feeling a lot better for it, but there was no movement, no real change. Moscow was the top and the top was stagnant. People had learnt bitter patience together with the art of looking away and they were comforted and cosseted by having, not much perhaps, but a little more than anywhere else. The country grew the food and Moscow got fed, it queued but it ate: Moscow talked perestroika but the workers, the people, the *narod*, they went on working and waiting and doing with less and less.

I do not wish to decry the art of looking away as I found it in my Moscow friends, their bitter art of patience, their raging docility. It is a bitter yet somehow admirable achievement to have learnt to survive, seemingly, without hope. If the public areas were dead and politics without promise, many people had still found ways of cultivating their spirits in private, letting their imaginative lives flower in secret gardens, refuges out of the public eye, in unconventional churches; places in their heads, in sixth-floor apartments, in books and poems, in kitchens, in vodka, in a delicate, glancing, biting, unbearable wit. For decades the people had been treated like idiots, yes, but the extraordinary thing was that not all of them had been convinced by the diagnosis. Without help or encouragement of any kind they had retained a seldom-spoken sense of perspective, of their own value. To meet such individuals was often a chilling yet also an exhilarating experience; to be able to join with them, however partially, in a sense of icy joy at having kept themselves together somehow, in having come through, was to be the privileged guest at a wake. And they do it by investing the demolished institutions with tiny signs of the life they once had naturally and spontaneously. Such Muscovites surprise and delight by telling the truth in unexpected places and unlikely ways, and sometimes they will do the foreigner the great favour of allowing him to observe them doing so.

For make no mistake, the great institutions are ruined, ghosts of their former selves: the State, the Church, the press, the law, the universities. Of course people, at least until recently, have pretended this was not so, not only for reasons of propaganda but because it is a terrible thing to admit a great dream has gone bad. Foreigners connived at this lie in the past and, ironically, with the advent of perestroika they do so even more readily now. But it is all wrecked and no amount of foreign compliments or pretence of business as usual will cover the cracks.

Go to the Bolshoi, as thousands do, and say the usual complimentary things, but close your eyes and cross your fingers as you do so, because the Bolshoi too is a wreck. Only the dancing survives, with a grim tenacity, at something like the level the Russian ballet traditionally demands. But the place is as rotten as the other great institutions, a domain of foreigners, big-shots, Party bosses on free tickets. The seats are impossible, whatever you pay, the sets are old, dreary and badly designed, yet foreigners, favoured provincials and the political élite mill about in the dingy lobbies and fight over disputed seats and tell themselves how wonderful it all is. The opinion of ordinary Muscovites is not known or sought. Why should it be? They never get to the Bolshoi: functionaries and visitors have conspired to pretend that such institutions are viable, that there was a law of sorts and industry of a kind, and a press that somehow deserved the name, and a culture that belonged to the people, yet none of this was true. The truly revolutionary achievement of glasnost has been that more and more people know it to be a lie and say so: not foreigners, or enemies of the people or anti-socialist elements, but ordinary people.

But saying is one thing and where Hamlet the Armenian is right is in reminding his Russian listeners that if the revolution never gets beyond saying, then Stalinism will have won.

The tenacity of the spiritual impulse in a society declared to be in love with scientific materialism is remarkable to behold, even if its expression should have taken many guises, some fairly logical, others as disguised, private, attentuated or perverted forms of the original. Poetry, of course, has long been a broad church for many. As the pace of liberalisation of ideas quickens, people are reclaiming silenced poets, and younger poets are coming forward to be heard in public.

At a crowded Palace of Culture a woman was reading her verse for the first time before an audience. Her work had been 'unacceptable' to the authorities for years because she wrote on religious themes. Aged about forty, dressed in a flowing shawl which recalled the young Anna Akhmatova, whom her admirers swear she resembles, her steady, round, rhythmical delivery sent shivers of pleasure through the audience. They nodded at points they liked, shrugged, smiled at certain images, applauded passages they admired; their absorption total, they seemed to fuse into a single eye fixed on the stage in an atmosphere of religious devotion, one great ear straining to catch every syllable. And she did not read but declaimed, seldom glancing at the lines, which suggested she had read them before, privately, to small groups, when such things were dangerous. Now facing the public at last, she confessed rather sadly that the time when she burned to do so had long gone. Above her, running the length of the stage, were two giant slogans painted in red letters. The one on the right read: *All Speed for the New Five Year Plan!* The one on the left declared: *Through Democracy Towards a New Image for Socialism!* They seemed messages from another world, far from the gentle figure on the stage, who adjusted her shawl with slim pale hands.

'What shall I read next?'

A man stood up. 'Read it all, read the whole book!'

The resilience of religious belief is perhaps the most novel feature of that tabernacle of old believers – the circus. You know you are getting old when the ringmasters begin to look younger. The ringmaster of the Moscow Circus was young and dressed entirely in white, a shining knight. The programme promised illusionists but warned against credence in miracles. It informed the reader, several times, that in life, alas, no miracles were possible; illusionists only pretended to defy the laws of physics. 'What kind of profession is it whose sole essence consists in deluding us?' it demanded sternly.

The sort of crowds which attend the Moscow Circus are of the order that once flocked to the Church of Christ the Saviour – and the reasons are not unrelated. The Moscow Circus is very famous and never is it less comfortable than when distancing itself from the old religion and superstitions. The programme spoke of illusionists who could make ladies levitate, bisected them, made them vanish in the twinkling of an eye and in their places materialised lions. Some even promised to walk on water. Legendary figures like the 'Water Dragon', a master of acquatic deceit, possessor of the 'Gold Wand of the European Illusionists League', had produced elaborate fountains on stage, cascades, waterfalls and sprays from 'God knows where' (the programme confessed), even after the city water supplies had been turned off. Alas, the master illusionists of whom the programme boasted paid the expectant audience the ultimate compliment, and vanished.

A certain Yevgeni appeared instead, a droll, appealing clown wearing a small bowler and a large black-and-white spotted bow tie. He led into the ring a miniature cart drawn by a donkey who was ridden by a monkey. The donkey attemped to eat the stage furnishings and the monkey attempted to eat the donkey, and it was some time before we realised this was not part of the act. Things got really interesting when the monkey leapt onto a woman in the front row, who played her part so well that no one took her for a plant. Her terror seemed very spontaneous indeed.

We watched as she allowed herself to be coaxed into the ring, and was directed to a cubicle from which she emerged moments later, glowing with delight at her reward, wearing a full-length mink and fox fur coat. It was only when she attempted to return to her seat that without warning the entire 'coat' suddenly disintegrated, turning into live minks and a real fox, which one minute was draped around her neck and the next was scampering all over the ring with the now near-naked victim screaming hysterically as minks and fox ran here and there pursued by stage hands with cages. Stunningly effective, and deeply disturbing, the act should probably be adopted by those who oppose the hunting and farming of animals for their fur.

The Moscow Circus mixed the shocking and conventional in almost equal parts: acrobatic skills, clowns, and dancers interspersed with animal routines using bears, monkeys, dogs, skating chimps, performing seals, horses, birds and rodents. There seems to be something buried deep in human nature which applauds the torture of animals, and there was some consternation therefore when one of the seals went on strike and refused, quite literally, to play ball; when the monkey did some damage to the donkey; and when a clown lost a hedgehog down his trousers and, for one blissful moment, seemed genuinely unable to find it. Next, a rather plump strong man in pink tights and gold boots lifted 900 kilograms without signs of strain and several bears were made to ride horses, with considerable signs of strain in both cases. Leggy girls put on a kind of restrained floor-show wearing Charlie Chaplin outfits, if one can imagine Charlie Chaplin with long naked legs. In another routine they wore punk hairstyles and danced of all things the cha-cha! The trio of clowns were delicate and punctilious and the orchestra at one stage played 'I'd rather be a hammer than a nail'. The children loved it and when the hedgehog set off on unexpected journeys down his master's trousers I thought the little boy next to me was going to liquefy with laughter. Yet something was missing, something was only half right.

The circus is at heart a vulgar business, like opera; but the sweat and sawdust has gone from the Moscow Circus to be replaced by science: this was scientific sawdust. What was missing, perhaps fatally missing, was spontaneity, the unexpected, the untoward, the unreliable, the unorthodox. The circus in Moscow remains a popular art – you can see it in the faces of the old ladies up from the country, the peasants who applaud the monkeys and hide their faces in their shawls when the trapeze artist misses his hold and cartwheels into the net.

The quasi-scientific approach which has tamed the circus in order to market it as superior socialist entertainment, equivocates quite hopelessly on the business of miracles. It wishes on the one hand to encourage wonder and delight, and suspension of disbelief; and on the other hand it wants to warn against religious superstitions and credulity. In short, it wants to have it both ways, and as I stood in the cafeteria in the interval, eating my slice of salami on bread and watching the children queuing for their Fanta, I couldn't help thinking that this place was yet another ghostly relic of its former self. The programme quotes with approval the remark by an Honoured Artist of the Soviet Union and 'Merited Art Work of the Georgian Soviet Socialist Republic', an illusionist famous for passing people through glass, making a grand piano levitate, setting a girl on fire and extricating himself from a variety of submerged sacks and locked trunks. The Art Work declares: 'The illusionist who tries hard to make a secret of his tricks is not right. Besides it is common knowledge that miracles never happen.' In fact, the contrary is true, as the rapt adoration of the audience testified, and the illusionist who says such things is finished before he begins.

Father Sergius, my guide to the ancient Danilovsky Monastery one icy morning, was a big man with a red beard in which crystals of frost had set hard. He wore no gloves but he kept his hands within the lengthy sleeves of his cassock and his crucifix turned buttery gold in the winter sunlight. Historian, scholar, his gentle conversation glittered with sharp asides, like knives in honey.

'After the Revolution came the persecution of the Church and clergy. Drowned in blood.'

Workmen were up on the domed roof of the Church of the Seven Ecumenical Councils, one of three large churches within the walled grounds, shovelling snow which fell in looping, powdery curves. The monastery was founded in 1276 by the Grand Prince of Moscow, Daniel, whom the Russian Orthodox Church later canonised. Father Sergius spoke of his exploits and of the intervening seven hundred years as if all had happened within living memory, with a regrettable hiatus after 1918, a period now rapidly being consigned to the dustbin of history. The monastery had fallen into disrepair after the death of Daniel, was restored in the sixteenth century by Ivan the Terrible and enlarged a century later by Tsar Alexis.

Father Sergius watched the falling snow. 'A few spades clear the impediment.'

The monastery continued to operate for a few years after the Revolution until it was closed in 1926, when it became a children's colony, a kind of penal home for orphans of people who perished during the Stalinist purges of the 1930s. When it was taken over by the State, its entrance gates were ripped down, its belfry destroyed and its bells sold to Harvard. The settlement that had existed here since the thirteenth century was quite unrecognisable from the outside. In the dismemberment of its churches, the new Soviet State was after treasure. Sacred objects were exchanged for tractors. God for grain.

'The Church warned the authorities after the Revolution: unless the treasures of the Church are given up voluntarily they will do no good. The proceeds gained from selling them will turn to ashes. We asked for time to hand them over. The government wouldn't wait. Violence was done. Priests and nuns were killed and the warning of the Church has come true. Nothing of value has accrued from the sale of Church property. It didn't save the Revolution or the country.'

Precious relics found their way into Museums of Atheism and Father Sergius tells of the delivery of a consignment of relics to the museum at Vilna.

'They were delivered in a state of quite dazzling perfection, a variety of limbs which seemed unnaturally lifelike. The museum was embarrassed, it was forced to display a warning notice beside the exhibit: "A rare case of self-preservation".'

Father Sergius remembers from the years when the church was still used as a children's home, a photograph which showed a slogan high above the altar: *We are all indebted to our Motherland – we are in debt for the air we breathe*. This will not seem so strange, perhaps, if one recalls that slogans of this sort were the order of the day. Children chanted, 'Thank you, Comrade Stalin, for our happy childhood.' And the infamous twelve-year-old, Pavlik Morozov, whom millions of Soviet schoolchildren celebrated in poems, songs and slogans, was regarded as a hero for informing on his mother and father. Children were as much victims as their parents. In 1935 the regime published a decree on 'combating crime' which allowed the death penalty for children as young as twelve years old. When at last the Danilovsky Monastery was returned to the Church in 1983, another home had to be found, at Church expense, for the children.

'They took their slogan with them,' Father Sergius recalled, 'and hung it up in their new place.'

The Church authorities have made a remarkably fine job of restoration, not merely in the tender efficiency which has been directed towards bringing back to life the fabric of the churches, within the grounds of the monastery, but in the air of lightness, grace and organisation so powerfully evident within the monastery walls. These are intangible qualities but there to be felt by any discerning visitor. What strikes one as stranger still is that these are not qualities likely to be found anywhere else in Moscow. Somehow the world seems to work in the Danilovsky Monastery. How paradoxical that restoration and spiritual values should make for order and good business, a rare efficiency in dealing with the world; how very strange to find these qualities not in an office or hotel or factory, but in a medieval church compound.

Father Sergius's eye fell with affection on the men shovelling snow from the church roof, a glance of distinct managerial satisfaction.

'Keeping the gutters clear, you see. All this is our own work. The money for the restoration was found by the Church. We preferred not to take anything from the government.'

In the Church of the Holy Trinity where Stalin's orphans thanked the State for the air they breathed, we admired an extraordinary icon known as 'Our Lady of the Three Hands'; two hands held the sacred child while a third, severed at the wrist, appeared from nowhere to form a strange triangle, an echo perhaps of the Trinity.

The Patriarch of All the Russias, head of the Russian Orthodox Church, resides in the Danilovsky, in a new house clearly out of keeping with the surrounding churches. For his pains the architect of the Patriarchate was awarded the Lenin Prize. 'I don't know if the man who gave his name to that prize would really have approved,' said Father Sergius. 'In any event, I think the authorities used plans for an embassy they didn't build in Portugal.' Next door to the Patriarchate is what Father Sergius in an unguarded moment called 'our department of foreign affairs', in fact an administrative centre which directs the business of the Church abroad. An enormous and rather reproving face of Christ painted on the wall of the Patriarchate appeared to be delivering a sidelong and extremely reproachful glance at the 'Department of Foreign Affairs', as if it had much to answer for.

Just outside the walls of the monastery stood a modest, fading, pistachio-painted church only recently returned to its owners. It should have been handed back to the monastery, together with all other possessions, in 1983. But the employees working in the place objected to the transfer, claiming that their work was secret. After much haggling it was agreed that they would leave, providing the Church built similar facilities for them in another part of Moscow. This was done. And when the Church finally took possession, the 'secret work' was uncovered: an umbrella factory.

'If you ever want to take something home from Moscow, a genuine souvenir,' Father Sergius advised, 'then buy an umbrella. You can be sure it won't have been made in Japan.'

By the time I left, the icicles in his beard were as thick as berries. The Christ on the Patriarchate wall threw his long reproving glance. Blood, orphans, umbrellas, icons, relics and fine business management; the Danilovsky Monastery was a very strange place.

'Is there any sign commemorating the children who were locked away here? Who died here?'

He shook his head. 'I would not like to see a memorial to the children. It isn't needed. Their presence is still felt. We welcome their ghosts, and the ghosts of the clergy who were lost to us. I am also against a memorial of the sort being suggested for the victims of Stalin. Do we wish to give the impression that remembering is limited to one person, one period? What of the crimes committed before, and after?'

4

Eating the Air

I began to depress Victor the waiter: no mean feat, when you think about it, because entirely of his own accord Victor had already sunk so low in his own esteem that he was in line for the free service offered by the Moscow phone company to its suicidal clients. His eyes, once dark and restless and hungry, had lost all animation and looked as if they had been cut from very old carpet felt, deep grey in colour and much trodden underfoot. He still hit the tourists for hard currency deals as they came down for breakfast, and his rates of exchange were competitive, but he no longer pursued them to their tables with new and improved offers. Such huge temperamental shifts are the stuff of Russian literature, but you do not expect to see them played out in a waiter. Victor's trouble with me was that, among my other deficiencies, I had failed to learn the art of 'looking away'; I was a foreigner; and my visits were not of sufficient duration for him to teach me about the way things really were.

'You always want to know how things work,' Victor complained. 'You have an excessively linear mind.'

Victor liked to fall back on this oriental strategy; the exotic country of the eastern mind, in which he claimed mental asylum when it suited him, proceeded, said Victor, by intuitive leaps. In fact, his only connection with the Orient was a passion for Bruce Lee movies, of which a cousin had a good collection. Victor was a third generation Muscovite and one day let slip that some of his family lay buried in the German cemetery. He was a lot more

European than I would ever be, though nothing I said convinced him that I was anything other than an Englishman who had been indoctrinated by Cartesians as a child and now could only think 'like a lawnmower'. Victor had something against the lawn-mower, which signified for him the ultimate idiocy of machine logic. 'You grow the grass then the mower shaves it into a desert where people are refused permission to walk. This is your logic. I say that in Moscow if you are to understand anything then you must change your thinking. You want to know how things work? Well, nothing works. Begin from nothing and go on from there.'

'What do you know about lawns?' I asked.

'A lawn is just upper-class grass,' said Victor. 'I have seen pictures of it. In *Homes and Gardens*.'

We were standing in the lobby of the hotel early one morning. Two enormous women had arrived with bags of plaster, buckets and trowels. Amazons, they towered over the guests. They had been instructed to plaster the little dry pond which stood in the centre of the foyer beneath a fountain which I had never seen in operation. The round circle of the dry pond always reminded me of a parched mouth. Victor watched the Amazons trowelling plaster around the concrete lip. I asked him whether he thought the fountain would ever flow again. He was perturbed by my question.

'I don't think so. I hope not. No, I'm sure it won't.'

'That seems a pity. A fountain that never flowed, a pool that never held water.'

'There you go again,' Victor complained, 'the lawnmower. Because you build a fountain it doesn't mean it will work. Maybe the water won't flow. Maybe if it flows the pool will leak. What then? Then someone gets blamed. Who wants to be blamed?'

The hotel guests were coming down for breakfast. But the glass doors leading into the dining-room had been roped together. Through the glass I could see the waiters sitting around at the tables, ignoring the guests who rapped on the doors and signalled desperately that they sought admittance.

'Why are the doors locked?'

Victor did not deign to turn round to look at the foreigners crowding the locked doors. He concentrated instead on the plasterers in blue overalls who moved about in the dry stone pool with wonderful grace, back to back, like dancers.

'Today is spring cleaning, so the dining-room is closed. Breakfast has been prepared in another room on the far side of the hotel.'

'How will they know that?'

'The hungry will find a way.' This undoubted truth seemed to stimulate Victor's thinking. Little sparks of life returned to the grey felt eyes. 'You're interested in food, isn't that so?'

'I get hungry.'

'Well then you must eat out. Eat around. Eat into Moscow! What could be a better way of getting to know a city? You must start with one of our great restaurants, the Praga. It's in the Arbat, I will direct you.'

I had heard of the Praga, one of the last remaining great restaurants from the olden times. 'Beside it once stood the Stolitsa Hotel I think? A bohemian rooming house where artists lived in some discomfort, a gloomy place.'

'There is no hotel in the Arbat,' said Victor firmly.

'Not any longer, perhaps. But in the last century there were a number, including the Stolitsa. It's mentioned in a story by Ivan Bunin, called "Muse".'

'Ah, "Muse",' said Victor distantly. 'It might be best if we stuck to reality. And Bunin – he lived for many years in France, is that so?'

I understood his drift. Bunin's sojourn in the land of Descartes had rendered him suspect in Victor's eyes. It did not seem worthwhile pursuing the subject.

'Do I need to reserve a table?'

'Just present yourself at the door,' Victor replied grandly, as if he owned the Praga Restaurant. 'It's State run, not a co-operative, so it's open to all. You may have to stand in line, but being a foreigner will do you no harm. As you may have noticed, we Russians are fond of foreigners.'

The tourists who had been locked out of the dining-room began yipping excitedly. A scout returning from the far side of the hotel reported scenting breakfast; the famished foreigners hurled themselves up the stairs in pursuit. The girls at the reception desk watched them go with relief, weary of having to repeat they knew nothing of alternative arrangements for meals. Breakfast was not their department. The doormen who had been dismantling the shoe-cleaning machine which had been out of order for days, now discovered that they were unable to put it together again and this gave them all a lot of satisfaction. The plasterers finished their work on the empty pool and began packing away their gear. Victor said he thought they had done a fine job, it really looked like something now. I wanted to suggest it would look even better if it worked but I remembered the lawnmower and said nothing.

The Praga Restaurant crowns the Arbat, honey coloured and substantial, one of the few buildings which continues to go about its traditional trade while the others are really only pretending to be cafés or art galleries. Once the Arbat quarter was the neighbourhood of the aristocracy, and signs of its former grandeur still remain. But it is popular today for its mall, or pedestrian precinct – the only one in town. The big houses, built after the French retreat and fire of 1812, have been preserved to give an impression of what the guidebooks call 'old Moscow'. It's a museum street, the painted imperial façades of yellow, rose, pistachio suggesting a curious contradictory impression of boldness and gentility, together with a sense of an almost outrageous self-indulgence; gables, pediments and stucco vie with severe neo-classical façades, and a row of trifoliate streetlamps, their round heads looking like rigid inversions of the balls in pawnbrokers windows, march up the centre of the street.

The impression of indulgence comes because so much of Moscow pales by comparison, because the visitor is reminded that this is what many parts of the city must once have looked like. The Arbat is special because it survives. The area attracts tourists in search of a glimpse of the way things were, and young Muscovites in search of the new. And, sometimes, conservative housewives who disapprove of old and new hurl abuse at the street marketeers till the militia come. The housewives do not know what to do except yell and point; the militia do not know what to do since no law is being broken. No one knows what to do with these 'new' people, who come out and show themselves on the street. Hawkers, buskers on the mandoline, holy men warning of fire and destruction, pavement artists, hookers, ply their trades among the snapping Nikons; wide-eyed soldiers on leave from the provinces stare at the wall newspapers with their demands for democratic rights; and the hipper sort of Moscow youth meet the pushers. Invitations to 'Buy your Soviet Kitsch here!' compete with the Temperance Movement's skull and crossbones, flying above a warning that 'Vodka Kills!'; and painters turn out air-brushed Euro-art, pink, polished nudes, a kind of fast food for the eyes which suggests that the gap between East and West is getting smaller, and that pavement artists everywhere are brothers under the skin, sharing the patent in identikit nipples, at home on the lower slopes of the *mons Veneris*.

The touts on the Arbat are always active in the wink and whisper world known as *fartsovka*, illegal currency-dealing with strangers. To be asked if you speak English or German or Finnish is not a request for language lessons; it is frequently followed by an offer to exchange roubles. The traders lie in wait for foreign prey, and often look like the tourists themselves. There is a law against this sort of trading and conviction carries a fine of one hundred roubles, doubling on a second offence. The police try to cope with the racket, spying on the traders with telescopes and sometimes also disguising themselves as tourists. Indeed, I think that in summer particularly, when tourists throng the Arbat, the authorities might take this into consideration when counting the number of tourists in Moscow because cops and robbers wear the same disguise. Fartsovka is a highly lucrative business. Present rates on the initial trade are around five roubles to the dollar. The bigger dealers then buy these dollars from the minor tradesmen, or middle men, and resell them to 'foreign visitors', as Sergei, a middleman explained to me, for up to ten roubles each. Undoubtedly these hard currencies appreciate further as they move throughout the Soviet Union and the Eastern Bloc.

I presented myself in person at the big doors of the Praga around midday and never got past the doorman. I was turned out into the cold among the small crowd of supplicants who can be seen outside the restaurant from morning to evening, like the groups of fans who gather whenever the British Royal Family is said to be near, or wait for the stars at Hollywood premières.

'It would have been better to telephone,' the doorman advised.

Several in the crowd outside agreed. 'It would have been better to book, unless of course you are a foreigner.'

I shared my disappointment with Victor and the junk-bond dealer in him stepped forward. 'Listen, I can handle this. I have a friend who knows someone who washes dishes at the Praga. He could cut you in on a table. He and I are planning a small venture. There are always more diners than places in the Praga. So why not *sell* the places. You own a place. If you don't want to use it today, you lease it for the day to a customer. Like opera boxes, or time-share apartments.'

'Do you know about opera boxes and time-share apartments?'

Victor looked hurt. 'I read *Fortune* magazine.'

'Never mind. I'll make my own arrangements.'

'OK. But capitalism is *wasted* on Westerners!'

But he took my refusal well. 'Why don't you see a film? I will direct you to the best film in town. It will cheer you.'

To go to movies was, at first glance, to enter the home of the deeply depressed. In the cellar a bar served what were called 'cocktails', a mixture of lemonade and ice-cream. The cellar was used for dances in the evenings and a young man was testing the level of sound from the speakers. He sat whispering sweet nothings into the microphone's ear while the audience waited for the doors to open. Kids mostly, soldiers, and teenage girls in bright red berets, boys in jeans looking worried and picking at their 'cocktails', platoons of army conscripts in oversized greatcoats. The loudspeakers hissed back at the engineer like a family of snakes or the background cosmic sibilance left over from the Big Bang. Everyone looked nervous. The threshold of expectation in public places is low; the longed-for enjoyment may never come.

The film I saw was called *The Needle*. A teenager from Kazan visits the big city and calls on an old girlfriend. (How Kazan haunts the memories of Muscovites!) He finds her in a shooting gallery working out with a pistol. She is clearly a person of advanced tastes. He moves into her apartment only to find that there is something wrong. He notices this when she turns up to breakfast wearing a Venetian mask. 'You've changed,' he tells her. It turns out the change has been caused by drugs. She keeps ampoules of heroin hidden in the fireplace. Every so often the pusher arrives and replenishes the supply, shoving the drugs up the chimney. The boy decides to act. He takes the girl away to the ruined inland sea of Aral, a desert where beached ships rust in the blistering heat as the polluted lake waters recede. There, in a deserted settlement, the girl fights to break free of her addiction, while the boy collects scorpions in a jar. Various lunatics visit the couple during this time but they don't stay. With the girl cured they return to the city where they must once again face the machinations of Mr Big, the drug pusher, and this time he has heavies with him. Before long the girl is back on the needle. The boy gathers up his gang and they call on Mr Big in the local swimming pool. He's wearing a hairnet. When he sees them he tries to drown himself but they let the water out of the pool. He imagines, and so do we, that the boys intend to kill him. As it turns out they merely wish to give him his clothes while, all the time, various announcements, unexpected and inexplicable, are made in Italian on the loudspeaker system. With his girl a helpless junkie once again, and Mr Big still preying on gullible kids, the boy feels he has no choice but to leave the city and move on. Walking alone one winter's night, freezing, he is accosted by a man who asks him for a light, and then stabs him twice. Though severely injured, in a final act of bravado, the boy lights a cigarette and stumbles off down the snowy path.

Most of the audience were under twenty-five and they loved it, and I could see why. The film, beneath its seemingly didactic, predictable surface, was an exercise in sheer self-indulgence, a very clever fraud. Pretending to illustrate aspects of ordinary, everyday life of Soviet youth, in fact, in the guise of being 'modern' and dealing with 'present' problems, it provided the purest form of escapism. It contained no reference to the debates about Stalin, reform or stagnation which obsess the politicians and the newspapers. Even the ecological issue, symbolised by the poisoned lake, was a red herring, like the anti-drugs message. The film massaged the imaginations of the young – if it was 'about' anything it was about how you wear your hair, hanging about, shacking up, falling in love. No wonder the soldiers in their ungainly greatcoats loved it and the girls in the red berets wept noisily at the end. It was a film in which everyone over thirty was a crook or a bore or of no interest whatsoever. Maybe Victor had been right when he told me to go to the movies. What I found was yet another world sufficient to itself which did not know, or wish to know, of others. Moscow is a moving picture show; when the pictures don't move, you do.

The very severe injunctions against enjoyment, and in particular public enjoyment, the lack of amenities, dancehalls, cafés, meeting-points, squares, hang-outs, backyards – in short, the absence of any places at all where naturally gregarious young people might congregate freely is without doubt one of the most bleak and formidable aspects of the city.

There are fifty cafés for the young in Moscow, all of them pretty wretched holes; many are places of barter, pick-up points, venues for selling American cigarettes and anything else that happens to be going, unofficial markets in flesh, drugs and consumer desirables. A video recorder can change hands for six thousand roubles. All youth cafés are in theory the property of the Komsomol youth organisation.

But there is a little café with no name, a pleasant, dark little room not far from the Pushkin Fine Art Museum, so deeply anonymous that in winter it is almost invisible, but in summer it may be located by the startling sight of three punks, maybe half of Moscow's small complement, dyed, quilled and studded, reclining on the short flight of steps that leads to a nondescript front door.

Patrons dressed in costumes which span the decades, from the quaintly old-fashioned flowing locks and bell-bottoms of the acid generation, through to the leather jackets and safety-pins of yesterday, taking in along the way expected amounts of dateless denim, and culminating in the sharpest looks of the moment, short haircuts, baggy suits, black shoes and white socks. Even the coffee is real. Not bad, if you can find the place. The café with no name is in Marx and Engels Street, a modest little thoroughfare, hardly big enough, you would have thought, to carry one name, never mind two. Reflecting on the anonymous café, Valentin decided that the authorities probably could not think of one which was appropriate. 'Everything pales by comparison,' he said, 'unless of course they decided to call it *Das Kapital*.'

Being young was a real problem in Moscow, he explained. Kids got drunk or spent time hanging about, going on the needle, studying to become vandals, *hooligani*.

'What's it like in the schools?'

'We spend a lot of time studying. Never have people studied so much and learnt so little.'

I quoted George Bernard Shaw: 'Those who can, do; those who can't, teach.'

'And those who can't teach, teach,' said Valentin.

Worlds within worlds within worlds; a society layered in descending order; the view always downward for what is above is kept from you and so you do not look anywhere but inward, to where one can be sure that you, and those like you, are safe; a honeycomb of separate universes, sometimes empty, always eerie, disconnected, yet somehow familiar. A society of societies, clubs, associations, families, queues, some of which you belonged to, some permanent and formal, some advantageous, some to be endured, others ephemeral but binding for as long as the association lasted. Those inside the Praga were one group, those waiting outside another. The two groups did not recognise, did not even 'see', each other.

These classified groups enjoyed, or did not enjoy, what South Africans recognise as 'separate amenities' and 'group rights'; just as South Africans would recognise the residence stamp in the Muscovites passport for what it was: a 'pass'. Some groups were more powerful than others but all groups were more powerful than individuals. Elite groups enjoyed special entitlements: housing, schools, shops. The Red Army, for instance, had its own theatre in Moscow, built in the shape of a star, located near the Dostoevsky house. But of course, what could be more natural? Accept the principle of 'group rights' and what could be the only logical outcome? – a policy of 'separate development', of apartheid, by which, in the name of freedom for all, rigid restrictions on the liberty of people to meet and mix freely are justified and even applauded as a revolutionary solution to an age-old problem: how to reconcile conflicting claims between competing groups. The solution is to deny that there is conflict or competition and to insist on complete freedom for each within his own sphere.

This natural assumption of superiority among certain classes is expressed with a freedom which bewilders the Westerners. But surely special cadres deserve special treatment? They were born to it, they get it and they take it for granted. Where else should a white South African feel so naturally at home?

The best and most exclusive group remains the family, and the fortress deeply defended is the home, apartment, or kitchen table. Here people may say what they truly believe, to each other and to close friends of the family. They believe, in private, almost nothing that is said in public, and what they reveal in so doing is the extent to which many have opted out of all the public and official parades of politics, patriotism, history. They have suspended their belief; more importantly, they have withdrawn their emotions, they are on emotional strike. They would have withdrawn their labour long ago had it been permitted, but then labour is a charade which produces fictitious goods. Emotions, faith, these belong to the individual, and if the individual declares himself dead to the State, much as ascetics once declared themselves dead to the world, then there is not much the State can do about it, except to rail and complain.

What is often taken to be cynicism is really disenchantment so deep it cannot be separated from despair. What was most valuable materially and spiritually, has been destroyed; what is available is virtually worthless. This means that, for the foreigner, the eye has trouble adjusting to the cityscape of Moscow and extreme difficulty catching the intensely felt moral anguish of private citizens. And as for the Party, it is so deeply discredited that even its members are reluctant to discuss its position in anything more than slogans and mumbled defiance.

I asked about a particularly handsome yellow mansion. Was it a school or an art museum? Valentin laughed. 'That's the local headquarters of the Communist Party. If your eye settles on any really good-looking place, you are pretty safe in assuming that it belongs to the Party. Much the same happens with goods and services. The Party breeds natural aristocrats who simply believe that there are certain things to which they are entitled. And that means the best. The best building on the block, the best health care, hotels, motorcars, apartments.'

It is interesting to follow parties of visiting Russian tourists into such big houses as are open to the public. There are not many to choose from. You would be forgiven for imagining that the only substantial houses left in Moscow once belonged to writers: Chekhov, Dostoevsky, Alexei Tolstoy, Maxim Gorky. It was a shock to spot a familiar face in the Gorky house, but there was George Bernard Shaw on a visit in 1931, smiling broadly from an old album of photographs. As that murderous decade grew darker, smiles dimmed and stopped altogether. The revenge of time has been to fix these faces in joy in photographs like this, the Cheshire cat smiles of foreign visitors haunting the rooms where dreams died; happy memories of an age of killing, photographic evidence that there were people who said that they had seen the future and it worked, who drew close to the infernal glow of Stalin and found it difficult to resist throwing themselves into the flames.

The little ladies presided everywhere in the house. They made visitors tie on canvas shoes and sent them skating over the bare floorboards to linger before the restraining ropes strung across the doorways of forbidden, holy rooms. People came, not just to see the artefacts of dead writers, but to wonder at gilded frames, oil paintings, candelabra, mirrors, paper knives, writing desks and Turkish carpets, costly relics of a fabulous vanished era which spoke more loudly than any literary remains. In the houses of writers people come to look at the pictures. What a chair! That vase! It is hardly surprising that you cannot hear the voice of the soloist in Alexei Tolstoy's house because it is drowned by the rich orchestral accompaniment of his beautiful belongings.

The only exception I found among the museum houses, where the spirit of the artist still seemed to inhabit the place, was the home of Viktor Vasnetsov, the old painter and teller of fairytales, who died in 1926. It is a Russian wooden house in the traditional style, built in the last century by carpenters from the city of Vladimir. The house seemed warm, naturally related to its former owner, perhaps because Vasnetsov's paintings hung everywhere. The most striking was his *Sleeping Beauty*, painted between 1900 and 1926, a colossal work filling one entire wall and showing the princess asleep in her overgrown palace. She has been reading and the open book has slipped from her hand. Bear, fox and hare slumber at her feet. The court musicians nod over their instruments; the jester has only just fallen asleep because his smile has not had time to leave his face. A beggar still has his hand outstretched though his eyes are tightly closed, and all around the palace courtiers snore gently. The scene pulses with colour and vibrating expectation, for the painter obliges you to look past the princess on her raised couch, through the open window and into the heart of the country from where one day, perhaps, a prince will come and kiss her awake. The entire painting is poised on this knife-edge of hope against hope which its surface fairytale prettiness cannot blunt. It is an image of aching tension, painted up to be just about bearable; there is nothing quite like it, until you come to see that other painted sleeping beauty beneath the glass canopy in the Lenin Mausoleum. How *deep* such images run – of suspended animation, hibernation, of dreaming expectation, of hope built on cruel disappointment; and perhaps this is why there is always fear of ice ages unexpectedly returning when entire species are frozen alive and scepticism of the 'thaws' which follow, and perhaps why life seems to oscillate eternally between eras of 'stagnation' and 'renewal'.

'We must always go all the way,' Andrei, the novelist, repeated ruefully. 'From hell to paradise on earth.'

The next time around I telephoned the Praga for a reservation. The place was beginning to develop into something of an obsession for me. I was not helped by Valentin's sceptical approach to the whole business. 'Take a Russian's advice. Praga means Prague – right? You want to go to Prague? Well the only way they'll let you in is if you go by tank.' In fact, the voice at the other end of the line was helpful. Naturally I might make a reservation for lunch: nothing easier. My booking was noted and confirmed.

I got there in plenty of time on the day appointed. The little crowd of supplicants stamping their feet and blowing on their hands outside the door remembered me and smiled encouragement. The doorman put up brief resistance, but I announced my booking and he gave way. I handed in my hat and coat at the busy, crowded cloakroom. The attendant gave me a plastic disk stamped with the number 41 and then promptly took it back again. 'It reminds me of the War,' he explained apologetically and gave me another. The solicitude of strangers can be terrifying.

I went upstairs to the first-floor restaurant. The Praga is actually a number of restaurants: the Czech, the Winter and the Mirror. In summer they also open the Terrace. The Czech is appropriately decorated with reminders of the motherland and warmly upholstered in thick plush. The beer, I knew, was good. A violin was playing gypsy airs. I thought I recognised 'Black Eyes'. The head waiter stood guard at the entrance with a clipboard on which my name could not be discovered. Perhaps I might try the Winter restaurant? I did and it wasn't; that left the Mirror which is really a banqueting hall situated up another flight of stairs, but that was closed for 'spring cleaning'.

'In winter?' I said to the floor lady.

'It's a mild winter,' came the rejoinder.

I went back to the Czech. Again the head waiter searched his list and failed to locate me.

'I made a reservation. I telephoned. I was assured I had a table.'

He shrugged, that inimitable, infuriating, elegant, much-abused Moscow shrug in which a spark of concern competes with cold indifference. 'I'm sorry.'

I looked into the room. There were perhaps a dozen diners. The place was virtually empty. 'Well, can I come in anyway?'

Again the shrug. 'It's impossible.'

'Why?'

'There are no tables. We are full.'

Outside in the snow the group of sympathisers was supportive.

'You should have booked in person,' someone said. A young couple called Nadezhda and Mikhail were concerned that a visitor to Moscow had been shabbily treated. She was an interpreter, he was a driver for official visitors. The party they were accompanying were ensconced inside the Praga and would be some time. How had their party managed to get a table? They had an official connection, Nadezhda explained. I thought of the dishwashing friend of Victor's friend. Maybe I had been too hasty.

'But I also have an official connection — at a Georgian restaurant. Perhaps we might all go there?' Nadezhda suggested. 'Our party will be several hours.'

I could see their point. Once admitted to a table in a restaurant it was sensible to mark the occasion with a long celebratory meal. So we headed off for the Georgian restaurant across town. The familiar queue of hungry hopefuls was waiting patiently outside locked doors. 'No seats,' someone muttered. 'The place is packed.'

Nadezhda paid no attention. A tap on the glass doors summoned the manager who led us down to a cavernous restaurant in the cellars, ceilings painted with scenes of Georgian folklore, blonde damsels and turbanned Moors, dishes piled high with kebabs and pickles. A table magically appeared.

At some point in the meal I made a trip to the washroom and was followed by a man who asked if I spoke English. Knowing this to be a question of the same order as the gypsy's request for alms in the Metro, 'May I ask?' — an approach which might be followed by an assault on pocket or purse — I came straight to the point. No, I was not English and no, I was not interested in exchanging currency.

He was a broad, blond young man in shirtsleeves, and he'd been hitting the vodka. He'd got to the stage where fuddled concern to hear another's point of view was giving way to aggression.

'But where do you come from?'

'Africa.'

I saw the disbelief cross his face and I sensed his unasked question because I'd heard it before. 'But if you come from Africa why aren't you black?' I took pity on him.

'From South Africa.'

The change that came over him was profound. I thought he was going to fall to the ground and clasp my knees.

'But this is the most wonderful news. Please, may I ask you just one question? It is vital for me. Sir, you see I hate this country, I plan to defect.'

I said, 'I think I must be getting back to my table.'

He barred the door. 'One question? Please? Is it true that Russian soldiers serving as advisers in Angola are paid a reward if they defect to South Africa?'

'I think I've heard something about that. I suppose some sort of bounty would be logical.'

'And if this soldier were to go there, to South Africa, are there other jobs he can do, besides being a soldier?'

'Yes, many things.'

'Even if this soldier had no qualifications?'

'This soldier would have the best qualification available in South Africa. He would be white.' Now it was my turn for a question. 'If this hypothetical person wished to leave the Soviet Union, why would he bother to go all the way to South Africa? Surely it would make more sense to go to Western Europe?'

He shook his head impatiently. 'That would be no good at all. In South Africa he would be able to kill blacks.'

I digested this information, praying that no one else would visit the washroom.

'Why does he want to kill black people?'

'He hates them.'

'Why?'

'Because there are too many of them.'

'What, here – in Moscow?'

'They're everywhere! In shops, the university. They behave very badly in queues. Most Muscovites wait patiently in queues. But black people push forward. Without regard. Without waiting. It makes me crazy!' His eyes grew moist, 'Sir, I cannot thank you enough for your help. Come to my table, we will drink a toast – to Africa!'

'Excuse me but I must get back to my friends. They'll be wondering if I've left the country.'

At the table Nadezhda said, 'In the corner is a man who keeps smiling at you. Do you know him?'

It was the defector. He raised his glass in silent tribute and mouthed a toast: 'Africa.'

'I've never seen him before in my life.'

'Probably a Georgian,' Mikhail snorted. 'Nothing but trouble, Georgians. Gangsters, crooks. They cause much of the trouble in the world.'

'Not at all,' Nadezhda objected. 'Much of the trouble in the world is caused by short men. Napoleon, Hitler – '

'And Stalin,' Mikhail cut in. 'The most dangerous combination of all. A short Georgian.'

Mikhail proposed taking me to 'an exhibition of the way we live'. Nadezhda returned to her charges at the Praga. Mikhail piloted his car through the lesser suburbs of Moscow in search of those domestic examples of Stalin Baroque, the neighbourhood 'palaces of culture'.

The architecture of Stalin was grandiose, the idea presumably being to create monuments which would inspire awe and gratitude, buildings which would say to working people that this was what communism could achieve: the common people were to be the kings of the universe, they would ascend broad staircases and walk across marble floors beneath crystal chandeliers. There is a rather brutal opulence about the palaces of culture, or community halls, built in many suburbs of Moscow during Stalin's time and used for everything from sewing classes to amateur drama productions. Most contain a professional theatre. The busts of the dictator have gone, of course, but slogans remain: 'Communists! We must by the force of our example correct and renovate the cause of socialism!' Emblazoned in giant red letters across the top of the stage, they constitute a kind of noise for the eyes which must inevitably interfere with appreciation of the action on the stage below. Time has not been kind to the palaces – the marble has yellowed, the chandeliers are unreliable, the best materials have not withstood the brutality of the municipal imagination that hated art but commanded halls be built for group recreation.

Mikhail also despised art and culture. He preferred his sports paper and he loved motor-racing. 'But only if the cars crash often.' He was a heavy, sad man with a kind of extra internal mass which meant you would never have guessed his weight.

'I can't spend my day off drinking schnapps and smoking, which is what most men want to do. I have to spend it shopping. To help my wife. That's what's called equality.' Like many people Mikhail had unorthodox views about perestroika. He wished people would not go on using the word. 'Thank God they've stopped talking about "acceleration". Did you hear the story about "acceleration"? When Mr Gorbachev visited a factory, he saw this guy pushing an empty wheelbarrow up and down. Why don't you put something in the wheelbarrow? he asked the man. I would, came the reply, but with all this acceleration I simply haven't got time to stop and load up!' He laughed and gunned the engine. The angrier he got the faster he drove.

Mikhail took me out to an industrial suburb where the giant Zil car and truck manufacturing plant was located, turning out heavy trucks for industry and big black limousines for the Party bosses, the favoured few, whom Mikhail calls big-shots, 'the Shishka'. The plant produced trucks and it also produced smoke and pollution, and a desperate dreary griminess which froze the heart. Outside the gates of the factory they had erected a truck. Highly coloured like a child's meccano set, and somehow miniature, it reposed on an altar of yellow bricks. The urge to enthrone is very strong: tanks, trucks and people. Over the way was a yellow head of Lenin. The falling grey sleet streaked his cheeks like the marks of tears. Everything was old, decrepit and sad. Many of the smaller factories in the area, used for supplying the giant works, were inefficient and had to be subsidised by the government.

'This is an ecologically negative area. I used to work here,' says Mikhail. 'The best thing would be to close some of the smaller plants. But they don't. You'll probably find that these little factories make modest objects like pens or writing paper, and such things are needed by the Central Committee.'

The flats in the area were slums from the seventies. Mikhail called them *Brezhnevski*, to distinguish them from the even older and more tawdry buildings which are called *Krushchevski*, substandard housing thrown up by Krushchev in the sixties in his race to house the workers. Both are now falling to pieces. Factories and apartment blocks stood side by side and people trudged, heads down, between the two. One or two forlorn little shop windows offered tiny pyramids of very small red apples. Only the liquor shop was crowded. Big, impassive men well wrapped, emotionless, waited in line and packed bottles into bags.

'What do they feel?'

'I don't think they feel anything,' says Mikhail, 'They've gone beyond feeling.'

By contrast, a few miles away new apartment blocks were being built for government functionaries. These blocks had underground parking garages, an unheard-of luxury in Moscow. Mikhail had thought once of becoming a driver for somebody important, perhaps for a Party official.

'The trouble is, the tests are so strict. If I were to apply for a job like this they'd want to know all about my mother, father, uncles and my grandfather and my great-great-grandmother. And who knows? They might discover that my great-great-great-grandfather was a monarchist. The way they conduct their tests you'd think that *he* was applying for the job!'

He took me to see the difference in standards between 'people' and 'bosses', a graphic example of workers' housing across the road from an apartment block for the more favoured classes. The workers lived in a four-storey pre-Revolutionary tenement painted yellow, the colour so darkened with time that it resembled old urine. The fifteen-storey tower across the road was built of straw-coloured brick and had a cheerful, modern appearance.

'I am a patriot,' Mikhail admitted. 'I was in the army for many years. I believed in the Revolution – but who would have thought that the Revolution which was to bring equality for people should have ended up by providing fancy flats for the bosses! Whatever the Revolution brought, it has not brought equality.'

The Party faces the same problem as that which confronts the ruling National Party in South Africa. It claims to be leading the reform, while all the time its credibility leaks away. Can the men who invented the command economy preside over its destruction? Indeed, if I were in a measuring mood I would say that the

South African National Party, the guardian of, and apologist for, apartheid, which God knows seems a hollow mockery of its former self to all who know it, retains a few shreds of credibility when compared with the moral and intellectual insolvency of the Communist Party of the Soviet Union.

Consider Yuri, an economist, a young man up from Siberia, ardent supporter of perestroika, leader of the international co-operative movement known as 'joint ventures' whereby foreign capital, technology and enterprise is wedded to Soviet labour, raw materials, and 'investment potential'. Passionate, impatient to the point of dogmatism on the need for reform, widely travelled and destined one day for the high reaches of government, Yuri, late at night in his kitchen, seems despairing. He is much concerned with inflation. It haunts him, he wakes up at night feeling it, he says, 'swelling throughout the land. Why do people not work? For very good reasons. If they do work they are paid in money which cannot buy much, if it buys anything. On the other hand, if they do not work there will not be the goods for them to buy. A stick, as we say, has two ends. These people here are like spectators.'

Yuri invites me to consider the emotions of the people I have watched in the shops. Besides impatience and frustration, do I not detect in some a kind of harsh pleasure at having their worst expectations confirmed? The shoppers, he suggests, are having a kind of hard fun, Russian fun. 'It is all a kind of show. A play. Words and more words. We talk of cost accounting and economic pluralism and markets. But what we get is State control and monopolies. Yet they demand that we be efficient and independent. Look at Hungary or China. There they have inflation, yes, but they also have goods people wish to buy. We have inflation without goods. The defence factories make television sets, the sets explode. Or they make antique machines and call them tape recorders. So we pay for spurious goods with fictitious money. We talk of new processes, but these are still directed by the central State bodies, new policies directed by the same old fools. Once they talked of socialist planning. Now they talk of cost accounting. When I hear the words cost accounting, I reach for my vodka. Let us have no more of this talk. Let's have imports, boots, shirts, running shoes, watches. And yes, let us borrow to pay for them. And let us refuse to pay for fake commodities made by spurious labour.'

What would happen, I wondered, if prices were raised? Would that counteract inflation?

Yuri's answer was to cover his ears. 'If prices were raised, or the rouble "hardened", what little is left on the shelves in the shops and warehouses would vanish overnight. The thought of higher prices frightens me. They say we will get this right, in time. But while the grass grows – ' Yuri broke off and gave his bleak little Siberian smile. 'That's half a proverb from Hamlet. Do you know how it goes on?'

I had no idea.

' – The horse starves,' said Yuri.

What is to be made of the contradictions? For Muscovites contradictions are not to be understood but endured. Consumer spending is up, per capita income is up, more apartments are being built, yet the Council of Ministers notes with some dismay that the housing shortage is as acute as ever, consumer demand cannot be satisfied and services do not materialise. Consumption of fruit and vegetables has actually fallen and in the Moscow region the cultivation of orchards is almost at an end. Where vegetables are grown they soften and fall prey to pests. Where they survive the pests, they rot in warehouses because of transportation difficulties; and where the worm does not destroy nor the warehouse rot, the surviving fruit and vegetables rarely reach the consumers, but go to special interest groups, and those with large amounts of money.

As the Central Committee of the Communist Party admits, the most pressing problem in the Soviet Union today is the shortage of food. The deep attachment to double talk is being eroded in Party documents, but the habit is deeply engrained. Thus: the Central Committee can promise in the same breath that all plans of the Party are subordinated to the interests of the people, while setting out firmly what the interests of the people are supposed to be.

*

Meals are unrelated to the food consumed. Consumption, in any event, is problematical. The interest of mealtimes is to be found elsewhere. One morning, at breakfast, two stowaways were discovered hiding behind the drums on the stage, a couple of sulky, sleepy girls in white tight skirts, who spat and scratched at the big funeral mute who dragged them to the manager. Yes, they'd slept on the stage. It had been too late to get home, too late for a taxi, the dancing had gone on until three. But *no*, they had not solicited the guests. Nor had they shared the stage with anyone. What an insulting suggestion! We watched in fascination as the manager rose from his chair and ordered them to await his pleasure on the other side of the door. There they sat, repairing their make-up and nursing their bruised wrists while breakfast moved by ritual gestures to its unsatisfying conclusion.

All lunches are long, since service is uncertain and the waiter who comes at the ninth call is as likely as not to explain, 'But I didn't want to disturb your conversation, you seemed so engrossed,' a reason as unexpected as it is endearing. So leave your table for recreation or exercise. Take a walk. You may well find the lavatory closed and the doorman, the attendant in venerable olive uniform, a green shadow in a darker corner, is not sitting inside the door on his old brown chair but is pacing up and down outside. He has become a look-out. The door, though closed, is not locked; inside, four or five young men are having a business meeting, money is being exchanged, a flask of vodka does the rounds, they comb their hair, check their diaries, set up their next 'venture' and look for all the world like young executives planning a kill.

Dinners which I remember with affection include those I frequently took with a delegate to the Supreme Soviet who was staying at my hotel. He dined with a dimpled companion and I fell, as it were, within their benign orbit. They spoke of love, and I signalled the waiter who came, awe-struck, at my bidding. The delegate was amply self-satisfied, plump, important; she was demure, pink, complaisant. The waiter must have taken me for the driver to the elected pair, or security man perhaps, because whatever they ate, I ate: smoked salmon and caviar, Georgian champagne and chicken Kiev. Was there some mistake? Who cared? Waiters drew close to our table and were captured by our superior gravity, our planetary importance. The badge on the delegate's lapel announcing his membership of the Supreme Soviet gleamed richly, a lucky star with which we were all proud to be associated.

'The hungry sheep look up and are not fed,' I suggested to Valentin later.

He did not think so. 'The hungry sheep don't even look up. They've forgotten how.'

I developed an obsession with restaurants: as Victor had suggested, I would eat my way in to the heart of Moscow. Except that dining out in Moscow was never a matter of food – if it was, no one would do it. Restaurants retain only the faintest memories of vanished glories: visiting Moscow in 1903 a certain Lieutenant-Colonel Newnham-Davis confessed himself delighted at the variety of eating places: the Ermitage, the Bolshoi, Moscovski, Café Philipov, the Yar and the Golden Anchor, all commended in his treatise *The Gourmet's Guide to Europe*. Alas, no more.

Co-operative restaurants come and go. A wider choice of food, reasonable service. But most accept only hard currency and are full of foreigners and mafiosi. There was once the Glazur, billed as 'the first Co-op of the Soviet Union', backed by a Belgian brewery, fielding waitresses who hovered above the diners like nurses, a white piano and the promise that 'the restaurant's cuisine shall satisfy the tastes of the most exacting gourmand'. It was the use of that word *shall* which caught the eye. Whether it would have convinced that exacting gourmand, Lieutenant-Colonel Newnham-Davis, I could not say, but it offered the *zakouska* buffet he so enjoyed at the turn of the century: potatoes and celery, olives, radishes, minced red cabbage, raw herring, pickled mushrooms, smoked sturgeon. The solemnity of the undertaking was a little disturbing, the dishes being served with slow ceremony and gravity and everywhere the sombre mood of stasis you may see in the meals for the dead depicted in Egyptian tomb-paintings.

But the Glazur was successful. So much so that the local mafia who pursue co-operative owners firebombed it, after the owner refused to pay protection money, and the last time I called the place was a burnt-out ruin.

Nadia offered to introduce me to a restaurant, perhaps the only restaurant, out of town. 'It's called the Fairytale – *Skazka*. You like fairytales.'

We drove out in the snow. Taking a short-cut through a forest of apartment blocks, we encountered a disabled crane which lay in our way like a gigantic beached and crippled crab.

'Drive on through,' the crane driver encouraged. 'I will raise my arm.'

We drove on through and found ourselves somehow *inside* the machine.

'This calls for us to rethink our situation,' said the driver. 'Having raised my arm to allow you in, I don't seem to be able to lift it again for you to proceed.'

'It doesn't matter,' Nadia said in an agony of delight. 'My friend is exploring our way of life. He will enjoy this.'

After some time spent in delicate reversal manoeuvres, we at last escaped the iron embrace of the crane.

'You see how it is,' Nadia told me, triumphant at this living lesson in the difficulty of simple things. 'The driver meant well. But somehow we always go wrong.'

More delights were in store. Nadia recalled for me the old patriotic song from Stalinist times: 'We were born to make fairytales (*skazka*) a reality.' Of which the intellectuals made the bitter, punning parody: 'We were born to make Kafka a reality.'

The Skazka, set in wooded countryside on the road out of Moscow, did not disappoint. Two wooden chalets labelled 'Bar' and 'Restaurant', bedded in snow to the window sills; both seemed deserted, both were closed. A shashlik seller worked his pitch by the roadside, catering to passing motorists, spinning the skewers of meat on his home-made grill, half an oildrum packed with charcoal.

'Don't waste your time. Eat here,' he advised.

I tried the bar first and from behind the door an animal gave a full-throated impersonation of a wolf. I decided to give the bar a miss. I banged on the restaurant door for some time without any response and just as I was about to leave a little man in a white coat and perfect black hair which appeared to have been painted on but not to have dried, listened sympathetically to my enquiry about lunch. Come back in an hour, he said, no need to book. He gestured behind him and through the open doorway I glimpsed wooden tables in a wooden room.

'You see what that place is called?' asked the shashlik seller. 'I warned you!'

We returned at the time appointed to be faced by somebody who might have been the older brother of our host. The hair was still black but thinner, and it no longer looked painted but stitched on, hair by hair, and his eyes were bleary, like glass tanks in which swam two surviving fish. No table was available. There had been a mistake. The Skazka was full. Falling into the linear mode Victor so despised, I reminded him that an hour earlier I had been assured that a table would be provided. Perhaps he would like to summon his relative? The fish continued to swim in the murky water. His relative was not here. His look suggested that his relative had gone abroad for a long visit.

Nadia stepped past me and took him by the throat. I was reminded of Gennady's encounter with the policeman. After a lively discussion, the restaurant which had been full found room for us. After another hour, we had still to place an order. Nadia asked for speedier service and the waiter turned to her with a charming smile. 'Oh please, you've barely arrived, don't leave us so soon!'

The food was surprisingly good. Herring, hot mushrooms and potato pie topped with melted cheese.

'You see,' Nadia said, 'at first we won't let you in. Then, we let you in – but we don't let you go!'

When we finally emerged from our lunch it was dark. The shashlik seller was packing up.

'Did you enjoy the fairytale?' he asked.

Foreign restaurants, I suppose, begin well enough, promising to uphold their national identity, but in fact all soon become fronts for creeping Sovietisation. The first thing to go is silence. Music, preferably loud music, is essential. It is the only thing Lieutenant-Colonel Newnham-Davis would have recognised. Dining at the Strelna in Petrovski Park at the turn of the century, the Lieutenant-Colonel noted with dismay that the stage was occupied by a variety of performers, 'None', he observed drily, 'of the first class.' This is an early and probably fatal mistake among foreign restaurateurs. Once the music starts, the place has been penetrated and it will be followed by all the other things: the waiters' relatives on the phone, the pimps using the bar, the dishwasher's father running a bank in the lavatories, mock menus and vanishing waiters.

Recently an establishment which claimed to be the first real French restaurant opened in Moscow. For a while it projected a charming Gallic atmosphere but then, alas, there came the floor show. Halfway through dinner, a man in a white raincoat with diamante lapels as big as bat wings, accompanied by three girls dressed as black cats, sings a song which even in Russian is quite incomprehensible since the level of volume makes you cover your ears. Next, a young contortionist dressed in red trousers and a white top walks on his hands and appears to be fighting the Russian civil war all over again, the reds against the whites. The reds, now as then, are mostly uppermost. There follows the rhythmic degradation of the floor show where the man in the white raincoat sings about hope, which seems an incongruous desire, while the chorus line reveals considerable pelvic ingenuity – girls who once must have had ambitions to dance at the Bolshoi because whatever impromptus their hips may offer, their hand movements reveal fossilised memories of the disciplined training of the classical ballet, graceful and airy, like traces of petrified ferns in a rockface. This floor show, like most floor shows in Moscow, breaks the cardinal rule: 'Never turn up the lights.' Swedish businessmen wince to see the girls age before their eyes.

Under the same revealing lights the musicians leave after the show, threading their way through the diners, clutching their spoils in bulging plastic bags. Entry into the hotel wins the musicians admission into the *beriozka* (foreign currency) shop with its cornucopia of American cigarettes, Scotch, batteries and razor blades. In their street clothes they look alarmingly normal. Even the bat-wing singer turns into just another Soviet citizen in a tweed jacket, his plastic bag clanking with booze.

The Japanese restaurant at the International Hotel claims to be the priciest in Moscow. This is its sole distinction. True, there is one Japanese waitress in traditional kimono, true, hot towels are produced and, yes, they offer chopsticks. But the waiters speak neither English, French nor Japanese; display lively contempt for the menu; advise against the seaweed; choose the wine themselves; and spend a lot of time on the telephone – when their nieces are not using it. The rest of the Japanese waitresses are Russians beneath their kimonos, and the pimps in the back bar are running a nice line in black market Italian shoes. True, some Japanese dine in the restaurant, but for reasons of militant nostalgia. Many Americans, deceived by the bright lights and the wooden booths into believing this is a pizza parlour or a Chinese take-away, wander into the room in large parties, wearing knitted bobble-caps and calling for Cokes.

I had a third shot at the Praga. Never say die, at least not in Moscow, and always keep your head warm. I set off, after phoning to secure a booking, and phoning again to confirm. The little crowd of well-wishers shivering outside waved encouragingly. The doorman gave no trouble, the cloakroom attendants took my coat and greeted me like an old friend. Even the maître at the door of the Czech seemed friendly and, yes, my name was on his list. However, there was just one flaw: for some unaccountable reason my booking was for the following day and the restaurant was, need he tell me? – full to overflowing. I could wait, if I wished, for a cancellation.

I sat down on one of the red plush benches in the corridor outside the Czech, with a line of other hopefuls. The violinist was playing 'Black Eyes' again. I had the company of customers I recognised from previous visits, all of us waiting for the miracle of a cancellation but without much hope in our hearts, when a man in a brown suit came up to me.

'You want a seat inside?'

I said I did.

'Wait here. I will speak to certain friends of mine.' With a wink he disappeared.

I waited. About half an hour later the maître came up to me. 'You're wasting your time.'

'Someone said he could help.'

The maître looked at me like an idiot child. 'A man in a brown suit? He's crazy. He just likes to impress foreigners. Never believe the man in the brown suit.'

Back at my hotel, Victor, the waiter, and his friends had been watering the breakfast tomato juice once again. They syphoned off some of the stuff from the great big jars in which it was bottled, topped it up with water and then either sold or bartered the remainder. People complain about the lack of enterprise in the Soviet Union. On the contrary, there is plenty of enterprise, the trouble is that much of it is illegal.

Valentin explained it quite simply. 'People who feel themselves cheated spend a good deal of time cheating others.'

Victor took a dim view of this moralising. It seemed that all hope was not lost. His eyes had taken fire again and the reason is worth recording. A market existed for video recordings of his cousin's Bruce Lee movies. Agents had been selected throughout the city and supplies sold in. Business was brisk and showed every sign of expanding fast. Victor was investigating the possibility of a city-wide franchising operation.

And what, if anything, shall I deduce from this? For what it is worth, I offer those who set out to eat their way into Moscow two guides, a lesser and a larger – what I think of as the Potemkin factor and the Praga principle.

The Potemkin factor may be illustrated by something which I experienced on the very first visit I made to Moscow, together with a group of writers. We were discussing literature with our Russian colleagues in the conference room of the Writers' Union and around mid-morning it was suggested we adjourn to the lobby for coffee. We adjourned, and waited. Half an hour later we were invited back into the conference room and the hope was expressed that we felt refreshed. The coffee was deemed to have been enjoyed, though not a drop had appeared. The Potemkin factor is capable of wide extension; what Hamlet called 'eating the air', for the air is 'promise crammed'.

The Praga principle states: 'A restaurant may be full, even when it is empty;' the converse also applies: 'A restaurant may be empty, even when it is full.'

There are several corollaries to the Praga principle: 'A restaurant may employ waiters to eat meals intended for the guests; some restaurants will not let you in. Others will not allow you to leave.'

And *always* remember – irrespective of the restaurant: wherever you may meet him, do not listen to the man in the brown suit.

Moscow has a way of providing a countering image from its stock of unexpected pictures to match almost every mood. Taking a walk beside the river late one evening, after being refused admittance to the 'English pub' in the International Hotel where they offer to serve breakfast all day – because breakfast had been 'discontinued' – the chimney stacks of the power station, white in the moonlight, raised two stiff fingers above the dark and muttering Moskva River.

5

Marriage Tables

I stood with Enrico, an Italian film-maker, in Red Square one icy Saturday afternoon. We were watching newly married couples making their ritual visit (a nuptial custom said to date from the fifties, obscure yet eerily touching) to pose for photographs at the door to Lenin's Mausoleum, and at the Tomb of the Unknown Soldier lying behind the impressive wrought-iron railings of the Kremlin fence, which is unexpectedly studded with bold black *fasces*. Enrico was in Moscow to arrange with Soviet colleagues a 'joint venture', the filming and promotion of a series of rock films. He had just been stung after engaging in the second oldest of joint ventures: he had exchanged currency on the black market, getting a deal for his lire so tempting that he had invested all he possessed in roubles. In so doing, and on his very first visit to Moscow, he had at a stroke reduced himself to the position of many Muscovites, a pocket full of roubles and nothing to spend them on. He was carrying a heavy plastic bag which he treated with some disdain, dropping it from time to time with a metallic clunk. I saw him kick it with the point of his sharp-toed Italian shoe. The temperature was well below freezing and Enrico was numb with cold and frustration. I wondered aloud what he had in the bag, but he would not say.

'But I had to buy *something*,' he kept repeating, as he switched the heavy bag from hand to hand.

It was a double blow to Enrico. He had been severely bruised earlier that day at his hotel when he discovered it was not possible to dial Rome direct. The receptionist met his complaint with a look of withering disdain. Nobody was permitted to call abroad without making prior arrangements. She ordered him to write down the number he wanted in Rome and then dismissed him with a nod of the head and the phrase all the girls are taught in a dozen languages at the combat centre of the Intourist school.

'Go to your room and wait.'

'Two hours I waited, and then I get cut off, after a few minutes!'

Enrico stared bitterly at the brides who were arriving in Red Square in fleets of muddy little hired Ladas. They fanned out across Red Square like moths, the snow leaving no mark on their bridal gowns though it spotted the grooms' dark suits. He was particularly fascinated by a short, warmly wrapped girl who climbed from the car and set off across the cobbles, lifting her dress protectively above her ankles while her mother followed, carrying her train.

'I've never seen a bride wearing a duffel coat,' said Enrico:

The bridegroom, not as well protected in a white summer suit, black shirt and silver tie, was shivering visibly. At the Tomb of the Unknown Soldier the bride slipped off her duffel coat and handed it to her mother while she and her husband posed for photographs. Then her mother slung the coat over her shoulder, picked up the bridal train and the wedding party set off smartly for the door of Lenin's Mausoleum where red carnations were laid and more photographs taken. The little bride was short and round, her dress was an explosion of lace, she looked like a plump, walking shuttle-cock. As they came towards us the truth suddenly dawned. Mother returned bride to the warmth of the duffel coat; the bridegroom's smile had set hard, frozen into place. The surly chauffeur of the rented Lada stubbed out his cigarette, slammed the door and took off across the windy spaces of October Square towards the Bolshoi Theatre. Obscurely moved, Enrico showed me what he had in the plastic bag: at least a dozen leaden, rather sinister busts of Lenin.

'She must be at least seven months pregnant,' he muttered. 'Poor little devil.' He kneed his collection of Lenin's heads and they clanked mournfully like drowned bells.

'She looked happy enough,' I said.

'Not her – the baby! Imagine being born into this circus. I'd rather die!'

In fact, it was wonderful to see infant Muscovites being born; a sign of hope to see them healthy, angry, full of protest. For this moment, at least, the odds were even, before normal regulations applied, before the world was too much with them. And the sight is getting more special; abortions have exceeded live births for some years past. Many girls are married by the age of twenty, most by twenty-one, flung from teenage into matrimony into motherhood. You cannot live together unless you marry. You cannot get your own apartment unless you start a family. Family planning is little practised, even where it is known about, and even when it is available the pressures are against it. Babies (up to five thousand live births a year) make their debut in the big Moscow Maternity Hospital where the tall, burly Director met me with an unexpected declaration.

'I am an internationalist. Although I'm from Georgia, I work in this hospital in Moscow without difficulty. Could this happen in your part of the world?' He eyed me defiantly. 'Are you frightened of blood?'

'Unfortunately, no.'

'Put on a gown and follow me.'

I followed him and so did his staff, issuing unbidden from each department we passed and silently bringing up the rear: obstetrics, gynaecology, intensive care; falling away when the borders of their territories were reached and others took their places: pathology, midwifery, labour wards. The Director glanced neither right nor left, down threadbare corridors he moved like a tidal wave.

In the teaching wing he suddenly flung open a door to reveal a group of young students who grinned and blushed and died a thousand deaths at the sight of visitors. A large model of the womb stood on the table, notes had been faintly chalked on the blackboard, but the demeanour of the students was one of furtive preoccupation with matters far removed from medicine; the air they breathed was of the boredom of the unattended class, of frustrated energies, of people waiting for how long they did not know, nor for whom. Had they been playing poker, rolling their pencils down the desktops, flicking ink at each other, or practising whatever trivial but necessary preoccupation distracted them, they were still bored; time stretched before them, dreary, uninformative and empty.

It was a glimpse of a scene behind the scenes. The students were not only shamefaced, they were slightly resentful. To peer behind closed doors was not playing by the unwritten rules, and, as yet, all true rules in this society are unwritten. Written rules, laws, are merely empty boasts or threats. It was a question of saving face. Alexander Herzen, most acute of pre-Revolutionary Russian observers, commented in his memoirs on the unfortunate tendency of Westerners to suspect Russians of being duplicitous, when all they were really trying to do was to put on a decent show, to keep up appearances. Thus the students resented being surprised and exposed to the scrutiny of an uninvited foreigner. The womb, the blackboard and the startled students formed, at least in my mind, a triple protest at this breach of contract between boss and workers. For this was not only a command economy, everything else was commanded as well. The basis of the command structure is as follows: I am in charge, you are in a subservient position (let us call you the student or the customer or the client or the voter). Therefore I will tell you what to do and you will do it. Or I will say it has been done and you will not – at least not publicly – contradict me. In return, you will be warned of my approach so you may go through the motions. This is called 'instruction', it is also called 'progressive', and I am afraid, in some quarters, it is even called socialism. You for your part will endure it if you must, avoid it if you can, despise it when alone, claim it to be the best in the world when confronted by strangers, but in your private moments you will wish to be left to get on with your life without the interruption of ebullient director or inquisitive foreigner. That was the pay-off, that was the deal, and by barging in unannounced we had broken the bargain. The real life of the Soviet citizen, of the Muscovite, I suspect, takes place at a subliminal level, beneath the surface of life; it is conducted in kitchen corners where authority does not pry.

Perhaps this explains something of the mutual embarrassment felt when, at the Director's iron invitation, I confronted two new mothers in a plain little ward. They looked at me with enormous eyes.

'Speak to them,' the Director commanded, cutting short my apology for intruding. 'Ask them whatever you like.'

The mother lying on her bed closed her eyes. The other was sitting feeding her baby and could not take evasive action because she had twins just a few days old and the second baby, wrapped very securely, lay on the bed beside her, waiting its turn at the breast.

'May you keep your babies with you?'

'That is not possible,' the Director replied.

'Is your husband here?'

'I miss my husband,' she said.

'The fathers are never present,' the Director explained. 'We simply don't have the facilities.' He waved a hand about the room. 'You see how it is here.'

I saw how it was. Not only were there no husbands, there were no men, besides the doctors, and no sister, brother, mother, father, or friend. There were no creature comforts, no reading lights, radios, books, fruit, toys, pictures, magazines or curtains, none of the small human touches that make such institutions habitable, no private possessions – no privacy. A ripple of shocked amusement ran through the entourage of attending doctors at my question to the feeding mother. They seemed to regard the idea of husbands in the wards with horror. Husbands had done damage enough. It was all they could do to cope satisfactorily with mothers and babies.

The mother of twins lifted her second baby to her breast and gave me a pale, frightened look, as if she had just been set an examination and might have failed.

The Director reached down and patted her shoulder, clumsily, but not unkindly. 'You are doing well. And your babies are perfect.'

In the corridor he said, 'Our infant mortality rates compare very favourably with those in Belfast, Northern Ireland. We have run a comparative study.'

I knew that the infant mortality rate in the Soviet Union was high; the country ranked fiftieth on the world scale, behind Barbados and equivalent to Paraguay. According to statistics published in 1987, out of a thousand babies born, eighteen die at birth and thirteen succumb before the year is out. Yet the big Moscow maternity home was, by Soviet standards, an efficient hospital. Though overwork had made him impatient, the Director's dedication to his hospital and his patients was striking and the efforts of his fatigue-ridden staff, some of them ghostly from lack of sleep, were superhuman. Even so, it was an echoing, forbidding place. A lack of funds explained to some extent the absence of even the smallest comforts but there was something else: the hospital was like a railway station, the women were shuttled through, the doctors there to make sure that the trains ran in, and out, on time. Soviet obstetricians have a reputation for being coarse and overbearing. I saw none of that but the attitude towards the mothers was brusque, at best a kindly impatience which clearly terrified some women, a desire to get on with the job before the next load was wheeled in. Babies were taken from mothers and returned only at feeding times. A shortage of trained midwives, whose status is declining for reasons no one understands, also added to the pressure.

The Director stopped a stretcher on which a woman in an advanced state of labour was being wheeled into the delivery room.

'Ask her a question. Ask her anything you like.'

'I don't think this is quite the time.'

'Nonsense. Here, I'll ask her.' He stooped. 'Are you happy, my dear?'

The woman's eyes filled with tears and she shook her head. 'I'm frightened.'

He smoothed her hair. 'Don't worry, we'll look after you.'

Her terror was all too natural. Many girls know little of contraception or even conception. Conceived in ignorance, born in anguish, nursed in fear, it is a wonder to see the babies apparently so unmarked, displaying the beautiful fury of the newly born.

The delivery ward was busy and noisy, the midwives kindly,

expert, exhausted. Along with other shortages there is a lack of drugs to relieve pain. The problem is compounded by a custom among Russian doctors which holds that suffering in childbirth is natural and women are built to cope with it. I asked the Director whether mothers were consulted about how they wished to give birth.

'Never. After all, it is the doctor who knows best.'

The woman who had been about to cry was wheeled into a small ante-chamber where mothers in an advanced state of labour, as well as those who had just given birth, were brought, a kind of parking lot or lay-by intended to ease problems of traffic flow. The women were lying on stretchers beneath grey blankets. She was in pain but her fear was the more terrible. She knew nothing, had been told nothing, now she found herself alone, on the point of giving birth, a trial which terrified her. However bad the contractions, it was nothing compared to her mental anguish. And the doctors were busy, not harsh but busy, and the midwives who were the most human and kindly people in the delivery ward were even busier. The woman who had been trying to cry suddenly succeeded as she was wheeled into the delivery room, a journey she did not notice. She concentrated on her crying – it was as if, having until then been in the hands of others, she had at last discovered something she could do for herself. So she did not really take in the birth, or the baby singing like a prima donna.

It was a production line and, after a kind, it worked. Yet there adhered to the ritual, like fossils in ancient rocks, something which dated and undermined the procedure. What made it old-fashioned were the signs that it had once been thought of as highly progressive, and it showed in the angular, jerky, mechanics; relics of the beliefs of bygone times, of the beginnings of the communist revolution, it still betrayed its origins, a soulless certainty that this way was 'modern', that science would take hold of human nature and bring it brilliantly up to date.

There was no one to blame. It was just the way things were. You delivered yourself into the hands of others; they delivered you of a child; they observed you for a while and delivered you back to your ward. And, yes, it all worked, in its fashion, but in making it work long after its *raison d'être* had been exposed as a cruel fraud, you lost imagination, spontaneity, sympathy, warmth, fellow feeling. Immaterial, disposable, they had been destroyed such a time back that no one could remember what they were.

Afterwards, the Director and I sat in his study drinking coffee and eating chestnuts in sweet syrup, a Georgian speciality. Since he was an internationalist I told him that something puzzled me.

'You use English equipment in your intensive care unit but none of your doctors has visited England, or studied the methods of hospitals in other countries.'

'There is the problem of money, of course,' he said. 'That's to say we have none. I've never left this country. No one here has been abroad. Some of us dream of it. Now there are changes and reforms. I hope it will come.'

'Why do you think it hasn't come before?'

He thought for a while. 'Because we were afraid,' he said simply.

The newly arrived babies in the maternity hospital do not know yet what it means to wait. They will discover in time, but whether they will be prepared to endure it with the patient fatalism of their parents is doubtful. Irina, blonde and anxious, a teacher, explained, 'We all wait. The trouble is I've done it for so long I really can't remember what I'm waiting for. Can you tell me what I'm waiting for?'

'I'm a stranger here, I don't think I can tell you.'

'Why not a stranger? No one here can tell me. Of course, if I think about specific matters then I know what I'm waiting for. At my school we're waiting for computers. We've been waiting for them for a long time. We've been invited to take part in a course which will prepare us. They show us pictures and teach us that way because we haven't seen a computer. Can you learn how to work a computer from pictures? We're also waiting for them to patch up the building. It is always in need of repair.'

Indeed that was the case everywhere. Looking at the elderly and dilapidated apartment blocks that litter Moscow, I asked Irina, 'Do you think some of these will simply fall down one day?'

'Why? After all, it took an earthquake to knock them down in Armenia. No,' she said softly, 'these buildings will stand forever. Moscow isn't a place for earthquakes.'

Then, in case her prophecy seemed too bleak, she thought of a consolation for me. 'But I do hear that earthquake activity is expected in otherwise seismically stable areas of the globe this coming summer. So who knows, perhaps we'll be lucky?' She turned mock-innocent eyes to heaven. 'The lives of the many depend on the decision of the one. It is engrained. I try to teach my students to have their own identity. They listen to what I say but when they leave school they begin to worry about it. I get phone calls from them and they say, "I think I'm losing my identity. What are the signs?" And I tell them – if you have your own identity you don't need me to reassure you.'

People are still told what they need. Irina would say this is an improvement on the days when they were told they needed nothing. But after over half a century of being ordered to do as they are told people are being encouraged to think for themselves. No wonder there is confusion. There is no tradition of independent thought; until recently there has been no permission for doing so and even now there are many who consider it to be a bad idea. If you project into the society as a whole the ubiquitous doormen and floor ladies, you become aware of an entire class of people who are seated very comfortably and who cannot for the life of them see any good reason for movement at all; deprived they may be but it is a steady, hard-won, familiar deprivation and has as its central advantage the knowledge that many are in the same boat.

Here is a dilemma: the initiative of the few must be encouraged, this is at the heart of perestroika; imagination, resourcefulness, business skill must be developed and rewarded. As a result, some will grow richer. But people heartily detest the badges of material success in others. This is understandable – after all, until recently the hatred of the majority has been directed against favoured Party functionaries who enjoy privileges in food supplies, accommodation and status well beyond the reach of ordinary people.

To those who have little it must be difficult to distinguish the new virtue of embryonic entrepreneurs. Once, when the plumber did not come and fix your pipes, you blamed the State; now you blame the co-operatives who have privatised the service and taken all the tools, and grow rich on the proceeds.

In the welter of words about political and economic reform, it is not difficult to forget that the changes to the economic order are still new and modest. In order to begin to shake loose the stranglehold the State monopolies exert on individual enterprise, the co-operative movement has been encouraged by the Party with a mixture of fascination and fear. There were, at the time of writing, under 50,000 co-operatives employing some 800,000 people with a turnover of three million roubles. Progress of sorts, in the first year of operation, but the infant remains sickly and its future uncertain. Within a year of its birth the State had acted to forbid certain forms of co-operative venture: health was to be protected; publishing; the press; the arts – all these were adjudged too important to be left to individuals. The result is what Arkadi, the government economist, calls 'cave-man capitalism' but which to the foreigner looks more like 'cottage capitalism'. You can, for example, buy flowers on the Moscow streets today where a year ago the State-run florists waved weary hands at empty shelves or offered you single geraniums at three to four roubles each. That remains the price in the State shops, but the co-operators hawk them for one to one-and-a-half roubles each. That is progress of a sort, but on a monthly salary of 200 roubles it is still very steep. Pay toilets, restaurants and hairdressers, sausage-sellers and house repair, are increasingly run by co-operators. But they are side-line activities, nuts and bolts.

Some of the smallest ventures combine charm and profit in a unique fashion. A girl at the Leningrad Station leases a pile of magazines on a penny a look basis. Customers crowd her table and turn the pages between trains. At the Yaroslavl Station, an old lady has taken up a job of story-teller to bored children. Co-operatives are on the hunt, buying, selling, swopping: nickel powder for knitted garments; wood carvings for IBMs; spruce bark purveyors, peat bricks, kilns and automobile servicing facilities seek partners. And hunting the co-operators are the mafia; restaurant owners have been shot, stabbed, burnt; protection money is demanded and paid; shotguns beneath the counter, guards on the door. There is little sympathy for those who fall to the wolves, police and hostile members of the public combine in indifference or loathing: 'Well, they can afford it, can't they?' And even more ominously: 'They deserve it, don't they?'

In an effort to understand what is going on, the wild-eyed foreigner seeks explanation; not from people in the street whose reaction is likely to be unprintable (a poll by a newspaper shows that a mere third of men and just 14% of women thought that co-operatives were an important development). So, then, it is to an official source that one must apply for guidance, in the first instance. Someone like a departmental head in the office of Economic Affairs, who asks that I do not mention his name but describe him simply as 'a bureaucrat'. The bureaucrat says, 'We are pledged to extend the pluralism of State-owned and co-operative ventures in Soviet society. What is not permitted, however, under any circumstances, is that co-operatives undermine the moral, social and ideological strength of our society.'

Now there are distinct advantages in coming from South Africa when one hears such orotund banalities. These are not phrases, they are the verbal equivalent of calling up armoured cars. They tempt me to enquire: 'What *are* the moral, social and ideological strengths of your society?' And the question is met with incomprehension. That is understandable since it was really a non-question. Morality, ideology, society are whatever the Party declares them to be. At present, with perestroika, the Party declares them to be forms of limited and controlled individual enterprise which will achieve the benefits of capitalism without challenging the primacy of communism.

And if you are so fortunate as to find an even more important spokesman, privy to the thinking of the Central Committee, and if he is willing to talk to you about real targets of economic reform, to actually put some facts and figures on these dreams, your feeling of alarm and wonder will only increase. If the facts of Soviet life perturb, then explanations severely challenge your sanity. Vladimir was one such spokesman and he spoke plainly.

'The practical aims of our restructuring of the economy is to aim for a personal salary of a thousand roubles for each worker by the year 2000; shelves loaded with consumer goods, electronics, shoes, dresses; decent pensions for our elderly; a flat of four rooms for each family and no waiting lists instead of four square metres per person as we have it now, and queues into the next millenium; hospital beds for patients who must wait in the corridors . . .'

'And how will people get these things?'

'They must demand them. They must wake up and claim their rights!'

Let no one say that the dreams of those who are the proprietors of perestroika are not ambitious. All this – *and* morality, ideology and social purity!

After this experience I went and sat in a café off Gorky Street where I drank tea and shared a sugar cube with Lydia, who came from Latvia. 'Moonshiners, give us back our sugar!' Lydia had problems and so it did not seem the time to ask her what she felt about earning a thousand roubles a month by the year 2000. Her mother was an ethnic German who wished to emigrate, as many ethnic Germans are doing, to West Germany.

'I live in Latvia. My mother lives where she always lived, in Siberia. It was quite a large community once. Now there are maybe no more than thirty persons in her village. Some live in caves. My mother wants to go but she is afraid to ask. "Asking makes trouble," she says. Because that is how it always was and she cannot change her thinking.'

Lydia from Latvia has more pressing personal problems. Her girlfriend has discovered she is pregnant and the boy involved has disappeared. 'I told her – what do you think will happen when you live with someone? Acts have consequences.'

Acts have consequences. But what happens when the perpetrators of the acts are controllers of the consequences? Or claim to be? Those who confer and control legitimacy are a closed circle still. But what of those, the mass of people, who live on the far side of legitimacy? How are they to wake up and claim their rights? To whom should they apply?

Learning starts young and lasts a lifetime. In the sandy yard

behind their apartment block one evening in spring, a little boy
and girl were playing shop. She was the baker, he was the queue.
He shuffled forward and asked for bread; she considered a line of
rocks on the ground behind her and handed him a small stone
loaf. He put it in his bag and paid. She shouted at him. He
apologised for not having the right coins. Then they changed
places.

Anna lived with her husband, Nikolai, an engineer, and their
two children, Nina and Maxim, in a modest apartment forty
minutes by trolley bus from the centre of Moscow. She was most
instructive about the domestic jungle of the streets and the great
and exhausting game of shopping. We went to the bread shop but
the queues were impossible, stretching into the distance. Anna
got pretty angry.

'It's the out-of-towners! They swell the queues. We're near a
bus stop and they travel in from miles away. This is a good bread
shop.'

Bread is plentiful and cheap. Its price was fixed as far back as
1926, but the out-of-towners were not there because it was
cheap, nor were they reassured by its plenitude, they were there
because it was there.

'If you think Moscow has shortages,' said Anna, 'don't go to the
country. In Moscow, we have something. In the country they
have nothing so the out-of-towners come to town. Sometimes
they make journeys of two or three hundred kilometres by train
or bus. They arrive with empty bags and queue all day. It's not a
shopping expedition, it's a way of life, a career. We'll come back
later for bread.'

When we got back to the bread shop the shelves had been
cleared. Anna cast an eye around the neighbourhood. 'It's ugly
here,' she said, in the same matter-of-fact way she was to dismiss
Soviet chickens. 'The snow helps to cover it in winter. Moscow
needs its snow. In summer it gets very dusty. I truly think we are
condemned to make things ugly. My children look around and
say to me, how long must this go on?'

It was Anna who introduced me to the talking chickens. The
chickens were dead but otherwise in fine shape. They came from
Hungary and were big stars in a poor, half-empty little suburban

supermarket we visited. Gleaming trophies in the plastic sales bin, they awaited eager buyers. Anna never hesitated. 'They're so much better than ours. Soviet chickens taste of fish,' she explained with that uncomplaining precision of the Soviet housewife. 'It's probably the feed.'

Even dead, those Hungarian chickens were superior. They showed it in the ice-blue sheen, their plump, goose-fleshed breasts. They had what it took to be big in Moscow: they were foreign, pricey and scarce. Shoppers paused before the sacred shipment the way worshippers once did before icons. To the Western eye they might look like nothing more than dead birds, ghosts of their former corn-fed, strutting, pecking selves. But the Western eye is often blind in Moscow, and the Western ear is deaf to the conversation of chickens. Get them into a Moscow shop and those birds as good as stand up and crow their heads back on. To look at them was to grow dizzy at their frigid hauteur, their barnyard insolence. 'We're here, we're fat and we're going fast,' crowed the descendants of proud Magyar hens. 'Get in now or go hungry. Or settle for our distant Soviet relatives, scrawny victims of some Stalinist poulterer, and live with the taste of fishmeal in your mouths for days. Around here, we're the equivalent of manna to the ancient Hebrews, wandering in the desert. Only we did not fall from heaven. And we're not free.'

No indeed. They cost six roubles each but it was only money and money seldom seemed in short supply among Muscovites; spending it was the problem – the unspendable in pursuit of the inedible.

As for redress, well, there are the promises but promises are to be made, not kept. The latest is an unqualified assurance from a government minister that the situation is going to improve greatly. In his words, 'In two years there will be feasting on the streets.' The derelict little Pepsi Cola kiosks with their faded canvas awnings and their shuttered windows standing deserted on street corners are a poignant reminder of what happens to big talk. You can buy pizzas in Moscow now, and if pizzas are here can hamburgers be far behind? And hard on their heels will come Western hotels and microwaves. But only the few will be able to afford them and Muscovites will shake their heads over these frivolities in the long queues outside the shops in the suburbs.

But what of plenty? – well, there is that too. Down at the Ryzhki co-operative market the stall holders were baying like stock-brokers, which indeed is what they are, retaining some of their profits in association with that great holding company, the State. Six varieties of garlic at the entrance, pearled opalescent heads packed tightly on the long stone counters. Meat and fruit beyond the dreams of local shops, at prices for millionaires; red grapes from Georgia at a handful of roubles – per berry. Yet how many millionaires there seemed to be! seething to buy, while severed pigs' heads look on with raffish eyes. Outside in the snow a lady was selling bridal veils, wearing them piled one upon the other, a flimsy nuptial Tower of Pisa. And the policemen were shouting down their megaphones, 'Citizens, please keep moving!' The dense crowds flowed through narrow alleys lined with stalls selling fake denim jackets at Paris prices, goldfish, cameras, everything, anything, was for sale – most eerie of the steadfast hawkers were lines of women, each holding up a single item: a passport cover, a pair of knitted socks, a novel, a fox-fur hat. A tourist took a picture and several people offered to buy his camera.

A public poll taken recently was revealing. Asked their opinion on shortages, half the people polled said they would never end. A fifth thought they would continue until at least the year 2020, and the remainder, as a laconic drunk in the wine shop told me, were 'either optimists or Party members.' 'Aren't they both the same?' someone else demanded. The shop assistant solved the riddle. 'An optimist is just a Party member with amnesia.'

Among the receiving classes the benefits of economic reform are most detectable but prices are astronomical. A new motor car like a Zhiguli costs about 12,000 roubles. You could sell it privately for 20,000. A used Mercedes will set you back 160,000. Bribes for better apartments run into tens of thousands of roubles. Attending this is a deep distaste for local goods, the fruit of bitter experience. A noted French couturier now making clothes in

Russia for Russians may find the cachet attached to his label vanishes. People prefer not to buy clothes they know are made in the Soviet Union. Manufacturers respond by sticking foreign labels on local products; the American connection is most powerful of all.

In the words of my singing taxi driver, 'In God we trust, and the dollar!'

A sure sign of new things: a rock star. A sure sign of the old problem: he has joined the receiving classes. And he and the operatic cab driver are united in their dream of America.

'Four years ago my group played in a stadium for seven thousand people and we were paid forty roubles. That's all changed. Today I get paid properly. And I travel.'

He has negotiated a six-year record contract in the West, will record in Switzerland and has fallen in love with California. When he spoke of California he began to levitate. He'd been there for a few months. What he didn't realise was that he hadn't come back.

'What I love about Californians is they're so like us!'

And if he was happy, how about his friends?

His mood sobered. 'People hate you. They believe if they can't be rich, then I should be poor. Maybe the attitude will change among kids at school. You should talk to some kids – if you can get into a school, an ordinary school, nothing special.'

Moscow schools are not named but numbered and all have a similar structure. They accept boys and girls between the ages of six and seven who continue at that school for a further ten or eleven years. My school was in no sense a special or favoured establishment. It did not cater for the children of Party officials and its suburban catchment area was what might be called Moscow nondescript. There were dozens like it, built in the sixties, with cramped little classrooms and scuffed corridors. The headmaster wore the look of a distracted idealist, battered but fighting back, a thin, nervous chain-smoker addicted to the immensely strong, yellow tubular cigarettes called *papirosa*. His ambition was to explore the bounds of the permissible without instructions from, yet without offending the wishes of, the distant centralised educational command.

I said it was a pity that so many good Russian writers were still forbidden to his pupils. He responded by explaining that until recently much of the teaching of literature was based on the principles of socialist realism established by Maxim Gorky and this inevitably meant that certain contemporary writers were not prescribed. However, these deficiencies could be remedied. There was nothing to stop a teacher from introducing his pupils to unofficial writers; indeed, a teacher of literature at his school had given lectures on writers as diverse as Nabokov and Joseph Brodsky.

'Then censorship remains a factor?'

The headmaster stared sadly into the middle distance as if it contained truths and complexities closed to the foreigner, and said nothing.

The teacher of literature was more impetuous. 'Yes,' he nodded emphatically, 'yes!'

And what about history? Well, that was more complex still. History, it seemed, had been temporarily suspended, due to unforeseen circumstances. Like the future, hidden in the upstairs room of the Moscow Museum, the past had also been 'closed for refurbishment'. The headmaster chose his words carefully. Because of uncertainties about the contemporary historical framework, no history paper had been set the previous year. The textbooks in use failed to take account of changing views of twentieth-century history. Consequently the history syllabus was undergoing 'revisions', a drawn-out procedure in which discussions were taking place with the Institute of Pedagogical Science, *lengthy* discussions. Once these were completed the new syllabus would go to the Ministry of Education for dissemination to the schools. Until then it was up to individual teachers to repair the gaps in modern history.

And what of the political reforms that had made a re-examination of recent history imperative, how did the pupils respond to them? He blew smoke at the ceiling and shook his head slightly, a faint echo of an earlier, huge disbelief. Liberalisation, reform, restructuring, openness – these advanced virtues left them cold. When asked if they wished to support, or become involved in, the political changes, three-quarters of the pupils replied firmly, 'No, thank you.' This indifference, said the headmaster, undoubtedly flowed all the way back to their parents.

At about two, just as the school day was drawing to a close, I was invited to meet the pupils. The mingled flavours of the corridors were of lunch, books and boredom, mitigated by the vivacity of the children in sky-blue blazers moving in chattering streams between classrooms. A roomful of computers was the most surprising feature, and strength in languages, English and German, being studied by many pupils. But a glimpse into the science lab revealed another of those places where children are sent to learn how to wait, a musty, cramped room with bunsen burners like drought-stricken flowers, the light from the window skidding off the green board and an unspoken prayer in the eyes of the pupils, oh God, let me get out of here!

Our meeting meant in fact attending a kind of clinic, volatile and rejuvenating, in which the students examined my political reactions, challenging and correcting any misapprehensions I might have had about the city – that is to say they worked hard to remove any illusions I might have harboured. I asked what I should see and do in Moscow. To get a sense of the real political feeling in Moscow, a dark-haired girl of about thirteen told me, I should attend the rallies of the democratic opposition movement in Pushkin Square, the only real force opposing the government. As the headmaster, the school librarian and several teachers were lined up behind me it was plain that many of the comments were being aimed indirectly at the school authorities, and through them at the Institute of Pedagogical Science and through them at the Ministry of Education and indeed at everyone responsible for the way things were done, or not done. Dull questions from timorous students were greeted with groans; conventional suggestions that I visit the Kremlin, the old quarter of the Arbat and other places suitable for tourists were derided as being at best decorative, at worst useless.

'Visit the queues,' a boy urged.

'Go into our shops. Look at the rubbish they sell,' said another.

A formidably articulate fourteen-year-old provocateur, short for his age but huge in self-assurance, invited me to see the new suburbs on the desolate fringes of Moscow.

'How can political ideas be beautiful if what they build is so ugly? Come and see where we live. We have nothing! No shops, no parks. Instead block after block of ugly apartments. This is the real Moscow. I've heard it said that there is a reason why they build the blocks a good distance apart. It is so that when one falls down it doesn't knock over the others.'

The applause was deafening. Then the champion of the democratic opposition movement stood up. She had heard, she began sweetly, that people in the West regarded her country as a totalitarian state. Was that also my opinion?

Surprised into frankness, stung into brevity, I forgot my manners. 'Yes.'

The line of teachers began studying their toes or staring at the ceiling. My questioner considered the answer in silence then, as if I had confirmed what they all knew; she nodded gravely and sat down. We did not mention the matter again, not the headmaster, the librarian, the teachers or the children. There was nothing more to be said.

The forces that constrict and confine their elders are something the younger generation will not accept. They are ferociously clear-eyed about the shortcomings of their situation and they are confident enough to express their views without the slightest hesitation. I learnt again that nothing a foreigner can say about Moscow begins to compare with the devastating honesty of its inhabitants. I am not saying that these children always express themselves in this forthright way, but having a foreigner in the room made some of these things sayable, his presence guaranteed a kind of safe-conduct for views normally expressed only in private. And I suspect further that the apparent lack of interest in the current reforms is not because young people are apathetic, but because they have moved much further ahead in their expectations and discount the current liberalisation as pallid. They want more and they want it now.

Perhaps there is something about authoritarian regimes which makes them treat people as if they were idiots. I asked Valentin his opinion. He thought for a moment and then said, 'Yes. And I find it harder and harder to remind myself that I'm not.'

There were also children who did not live at home, did not go to a normal school, children like those who had once occupied the Danilovsky Monastery and thanked the State for the air they breathed. I set off to find them, though my friends were not encouraging. 'Why do you want to do that? It's not enriching,' Valentin warned.

The place itself might have been a library or a railway station or an aeroplane hangar, which the kids inhabited like swirling, nimble ghosts. In fact, it was a home, a State boarding school for children who had been taken into care. There were about forty or fifty children living there, separated from their parents for a variety of reasons: they had been beaten or abused; their parents were incompetent or alcoholic, or used drugs. It was a place of safety, at least in theory; children might sometimes be permitted to see their parents at weekends.

Lilya and Lena were eight and nine respectively and took me on a tour.

'It's awful,' said Lena.

'I hate the boys,' whispered Lilya.

Both clutched soft toys. Lena was clearly the leader, and scorned the boys who fired imaginary pistols and blew smoke from their fingers. The girls led the way, hugging their toys to their chests, in thin cotton dresses, wise little faces and the ways of thirty-year-olds. The boys followed, they owned nothing but their bravado, and together we traipsed through empty rooms; a smell of dust, plastic, old food and unwashed bedding. The boys fought with the girls, Lilya complained, and the girls were forced to fight back. The children ate, slept, quarrelled, wept in this place, and much of the time they did so alone. Valentin had been right – it was not enriching.

'Excuse me, sir.' A little boy appeared at my elbow. 'Do you have any non-Soviet chewing gum?'

Lilya showed me their dormitories. Rank, unwashed, unswept. Bare, dark rooms with high ceilings. The skinny mattresses had slipped from the iron bedsteads. They had the makeshift look of a refugee camp – or camp beds in a railway station, or cellar. Lena slept with a grey woollen donkey she had found in the street. One ear had been torn off and its face had faded to a single nostril and half an eye.

Adults were scarce after dark: an old woman on the distant door and two voluntary workers. Christian volunteers and charity are ideas only recently permitted, for the State is expected to care for these children – and in its own way it does: they are clothed and fed. The teachers, who are State employees, leave at the end of the school day and two voluntary workers take over, play games with the children, read to them, make tea and keep them company until bedtime. A third rota of volunteers arrive when the children are in bed and watch through the night.

'Excuse me, sir,' said another little boy, 'have you brought us more orphans from Armenia?'

Lilya and Lena brushed him off and our tour continued. Lena showed me what she called 'our hall', a sort of waiting room with a table, a weak little light and a map of the world with the Eastern Bloc countries marked in red, rather like the old maps of the British Empire.

'Over on the wall is our political map,' said Lena. 'And here is our noticeboard.'

A note on the noticeboard was written in a firm, looping hand in a blue biro on a scrap of lined paper: *Someone has lost a packet of twelve needles. The person who has lost the needles asks the person who took them to return them.* Beside the note were clippings from newspapers showing the arrival home of young soldiers from Afghanistan. Upon the wall was a portrait of Lenin and he was smiling: this was Lenin the kindly uncle.

The volunteers try hard but they are few, and the children are many and wild, and anyway it is only the youngest who can still be helped. The others are moving away: down in the cold entrance hall the fourteen-year-olds are clustered around the only phone; outside in the dark yard the seventeen-year-olds are glued to a portable cassette player and lift disconsolate, suspicious faces at the first sign of an adult.

Lena and Lilya tugged at their thin frocks, turned pinched, anxious faces and confided that they missed their mothers, wished they were home, as if by whispering their hearts' dream to a stranger they might bring about the longed-for miracle.

Moscow has many attitudes; whorish, hangdog, sullen, then suddenly under a good snowfall it brightens as if freshly painted. On a good summer's day it can seem almost welcoming, a sudden smile from a dusty doorway. This morning, in early spring, it is covered in grey mist, sluggish, pretending to be some grimy industrial town tired of itself and sick of its factories; the last little coverings of snow are thinning fast to show the black, sodden mud.

Dip beneath the outer ring road which circles Moscow like a concrete noose, and immediately it feels easier to breathe. Within the city boundaries the lack of colour, of variety, of anything disuniform, piebald, skew, flamboyant or even the faintest bit florid, strikes like a chill in the heart. And the concrete. Apartment blocks dominate the disconsolate acres on the out-skirts more brutally than elsewhere. But just beyond the city limits, they vanish abruptly and there are fields, patches of woodland and painted wooden houses. They stand in their own grounds, simple places, a strip of earth, a tree, peeling paint and warping timbers, but houses, carved, curved, painted pink, pistachio, indigo, marine blue, some with their windows, others with their eaves, frosted like wedding cakes, or frothing like lace. There they stand, particularly in what I suppose I must call the peri-urban areas, like flowers among the forest of concrete trees where most people roost. The houses represent a memory of organic growth while the concrete triffids towering above them represent somebody's dream of the future. Well, if I have seen the future then it hurts.

It is the shapely, imaginative individuality of the houses which is so refreshing; the way that the wood has been worked, shaped, scalloped, stepped; and the love of strong colour, the basic shades in which the houses are painted and the variety of hues employed for contrast and decoration; the windows and their surrounds are picked out in white, red, blue or green, in dotted, stippled or chevron patterns. The effect is both complex and charming and the paints are used rather like eye make-up, to frame and emphasise the windows. Colour is an enormous relief to the eye after the grey-green concrete high-rise apartment buildings in which the outer swathes of Moscow are grimly entombed, brutal testaments to the city's incapacity to house its inhabitants in anything but dreary tower blocks, when it manages to house them at all. But there is no place for sentiments of this sort. Behind the little houses loom the tower blocks. And that is where the occupiers of these old dwellings wish to be – away from the outside toilet, the draughts and leaks, into the security of the high-rise hutch.

Define, confine, consign appears to have been the programme for many years; by group, class, suburb, job. You may be known by where you live; you may be known by what you are called. Unlike the choice of housing, here the possibilities are many. The various forms of insult available, particularly political insults, are rich and educative. You can be numbered along the spiritual heirs of Dan and Martov, which is to be accused of being a follower of the Mensheviks or of Russian Social Democracy; you can be called a spiritual follower of Trotsky and Yagoda (the feared head of Stalin's secret police, who was replaced by Yeshov, known as the poisonous dwarf, and Yeshov in turn was replaced by Beria, perhaps the most murderous of them all); you may be dubbed a NEPman which means that you believed (wrongly) in Lenin's New Economic Policy; or you can be called a Basmatch or a kulak, meaning a rich peasant. And if someone asks to which 'lodge' you belong, the sneering suggestion is that you are Jewish. Belief in a sinister link between Jews and masons is very strong.

Underlying this sort of verbal bullying is the belief that such weapons will move people; and underpinning that idea is the conviction that people are unable to move themselves. At present, history is being stood on its head, and those eager for reform to be led by the Party have latterly discovered that Lenin argued that people should be obliged to be independent. Things went wrong when they were compelled by Stalin and others to be obedient. The problem really is not that they were made to be one thing or the other but that they were compelled at all. Among those most addicted to compulsion are the economists. Once the people were to strive to be heroes of labour, now they are to become producers and consumers. Small wonder many Muscovites have gone into hiding, deep within themselves.

An excursion to the USSR Exhibition of Economic Achievement reveals a park of 553 acres with pavilions claiming architectural cousinage with the styles of various Soviet republics, and several others exclusively given over to general themes like science and space and consumer goods. You are greeted by a vast triumphal entrance, a fine example of Stalin Baroque, all columns and spikes and pillars, and high up on the pediment gigantic gilded figures of a man and a woman holding aloft the promised cornucopia in the shape of a sheaf of corn. It seems the destiny of the majority is to be mocked by their monuments. But people fight back and when the temperature is minus 15 the pavilions often serve a purpose other than simply exhibiting the economic prowess of the country: they are heated and offer shelter among displays of meringues, milk-bottles, river-boats, chocolates, lemonade, cocktail snacks, coriander, cloves and turmeric, fabrics, computers and bearings. Instructional courses to a grateful populace, lessons in stone and steel and glass, concrete assurances, living proof that things are working. Why then do the meringues lie in their bowl like mutant mushrooms? Less than ever do they seem to justify their extravagant name, snowy, sugary, airy confections filled with cream. But is that not what meringues are supposed to be? Not these leaden little cowpats.

'Plaster of Paris,' said Valentin.

Plaster of Paris meringues; artificial bottled milk, that is why it looked granulated, it knew no cow, a closely packed collection of white pellets; and the river-boats were shells; the chocolates antique beyond memory; the lemonade was not; the cocktail snacks merely boxes with pictures on them; the spices had no memory of the Orient; the fabrics are unobtainable; the computers a distant rumour, and everyone had lost their bearings. But what was this? Three books, all about half an inch thick, bound in bright covers and reposing beneath a perspex bubble. The title of these works announces them to be 'Measures Aimed at Implementing the Quality of the District System of Management' for 1980 and 1983 and 1987.

The most modern pavilion, with a stepped roof and its own entrance arch, holds the latest and the best in Soviet technology and consumer goods, video games, children's toys – a few examples of each, like the things they put in time capsules to excite future generations – electric organs and guitars, lounge suites and refrigerators. There is a kind of logic behind this need to put the brightest and the best into a museum; it is a way of preserving excellence but also of asserting the existence of pianos, unexceptional refrigerators and large cassette recorders, modest, perhaps, yet priceless since they are to be found nowhere else. Consumer goods live in reservations, in museums, in glass cases, to be admired but never touched. Curious that a philosophy dedicated to the ownership of goods in community should have made much untouchable, and so little available. A museum is a transparent grave, it requires considerable ingenuity and self-confidence if it is to imitate life, particularly if the exhibits exist nowhere else. Foreign museums often house what has ceased to exist; Soviet consumer museums house what is still to come – they seem designed to tantalise or merely to sadden the viewer.

I am left with the memory of a large photograph of a wonderful supermarket, its shelves stuffed with food, cash tills on the check-out desks ready for customers. People came and stared at the photograph. That supermarket was not there to be used, it was there to be admired.

A caption beneath the photograph read: *How Social Problems Are Solved on the Level of the Districts.*

They were restacking the Coke machine in the hotel lobby. The door of the machine was open, the area had been roped off to keep back the crowd and two men were on their knees in front of the machine while a woman peered over their shoulders as they solemnly transferred cans of Coke from boxes into the shelves of the machine. It was not a commercial transaction, it was not a chore, it was a kind of sacred act. All onlookers were keeping well back, behind the rope – or was it white tape, the sort that police put up after serious accidents or bomb blasts? Whatever it was, it kept the curious at bay, they did not dare cross the sacred boundaries but looked on quietly, respectfully, as the red cans passed from hand to hand and disappeared into the machine. There was something mysterious about it, the hungry machine, the yawning door, the much prized cans of Coca Cola (not Pepsi, which is sometimes sold in the kiosks on the street). This was the real thing, cans of Coke, in smart red jackets the colour of Santa Claus, icons of capitalism. No wonder people were excited, reverent, even awe-struck. It tasted good, it was foreign, and it came from an obedient machine; put in your money and out came the spanking cans, delectable and barber-pole bright. The machine did not ask you your name or send you to the back of the queue. It is not surprising that people spent hours among automata.

An international exhibition of automata was taking place in a hall set in a great forest of birches, within the city but some distance from the centre.

I'd been invited by a government economist named Vladimir, a rising star in the group which advises the government on modern methods.

'The trouble is that we know the prices of things but not their cost. Knowing the price of something but not its cost is rather like a young man who wishes to have his way with a girl but cannot find her waist.' He thought for a moment. 'We are surely not a nation of idiots.'

Many of the automata seemed to be misbehaving. There was, for instance, the Rocotron, otherwise known as a brush robot. It had come to a complete stop, the rollers which feed a copper plate through the machine had seized up, and an earnest young man in a blue suit was cleaning the rollers with a tin labelled ersatz turpentine. A computer played chess with itself.

Not far away was an automaton attributed to somebody called John Brown, an adjunct of something called Trafalgar House. The very pukka sonic assertion of all the names made it British right down to its gaiters. It was popular among the Russians, the crowds were three deep. The automaton was attempting to set small blocks of red plastic into a circuit board. The yellow arm worked tirelessly fetching bits of plastic, moving with a confident pluck and swoop from its box of supplies to a point just above the circuit board, and then with a little darting movement planted the bright red plastic counter into a corner of the board. That at least was the theory, but the machine was wild and even wilful. I could tell that from the expression on the face of the man minding it. He wore a British suit, a British moustache and a very British air of exasperation. He looked at the machine as one might at an incompetent foreigner attempting some elementary British manoeuvre and failing, like changing trains at Kings Cross or ignoring a zebra crossing. The machine believed that once it had deposited its four little square red counters at each corner of the circuit board it must remove them and drop them in a circular wastepaper bin to the left of the board. This meant its keeper had to retrieve the little red bits from the wastepaper bin and put them into the circuit board by hand, trying of course to keep pace with the confident rhythmical application of the automated arm. The Russians looked on with approval. They liked the considerable human input, men acting as a link between the theory of the design and the imperfect practice of the machine. Increasing automation, at least on that level, would certainly not lead to unemployment. Its keeper made several adjustments to the machine which the automated arm accepted with a hiss of compressed air, rather like a long-suffering sigh, and promptly added a new dimension to the game. It began dropping the plastic blocks some inches away from the bin. Clearly word was spreading among the automata and the mechanical circuit-board builder had picked up its bad habits from the unreliable Rocotron brush robot.

The Russians stood around carrying armfuls of free publicity material, shining examples of the automata of tomorrow, fat and glossy productions of the publicist's art. Some had eight or nine brochures, some of them were clearly there for the brochures alone. There was an air of holiday, of bright good spirits. Foreigners were giving away pretty pictures and glistening magazines for nothing. Across the way a Mitsubishi computer was making beautiful patterns on its screen, a line of spokes rather like pick-up sticks which fanned, curved, flowed towards the eye like multi-coloured waves, breaking and receding again. A notice beneath it advised, *Press Any Key to Regenerate.*

The chess-playing computer had stopped playing after the opening moves. White and black had each moved a pawn and a knight and then I suppose it must have lost interest.

The Germans had pitched a hospitality marquee inside the building and were helping prospective Soviet clients to coffee and cognac. After some hours they would very carefully help them out again. Enormous photographs of the German Chancellor, Gorbachev and Sakharov, beamed down as Russians and Germans, arm in arm, wove unsteadily out of the tent shouting jocular directions to the lavatories.

These were in the basement, tiled in a very serviceable black, built at about the time of the Revolution and seldom cleaned or repaired since. Several of the urinals were 'closed'. This was indicated by draping a sheet of newspaper over them. The toilet paper was placed in single sheets on a table at the entrance, like raffle tickets.

Some time later I mentioned to Valentin that the toilets probably pre-dated the Revolution.

Valentin gave a cold smile. 'Not at all.'

'How do you know that? Have you seen them?'

'No, but I know immediately from that description that they are modern. If they'd been built before the Revolution they would have worked.'

Press any key to regenerate.

A room where someone had saved a piece of pottery, a painting, a piece of glass, a few books, icons from earlier times. Treasures, relics, a glimpse of the quality of life some once took for granted, in the gleam of a tortoiseshell frame, in the curve of a table, that plump important vase, queening it over the room in its portly, secret shine, the fluting of a table leg, that painting which shows a road running through a village leading into the world before this one.

In her bedsitting room Natalya waited to give me tea. She lived in what is called a 'communal flat' with several other families, sharing a kitchen, bathroom and lavatory. In the thirties Natalya married an American who came to the Soviet Union because, as she says, 'the poor fellow believed in building socialism . . .' Her eyebrows went up, she smoothed her very elegant bottle-green dress and shook her head slowly as if still unable to contain her incredulity at the strange ambition of her American husband. 'Of course there were problems. He was married when he came here and his wife followed him from America. But she didn't like it. I think she saw a few pictures of me and that decided her. She left. She went back to America. And so we got married. But first he had to become a Soviet citizen. Those were difficult times, Stalin was in charge and we had very little freedom. In order to marry me he had to take out citizenship and so he did.' Natalya's hair was still red, rather well dyed, and her dress was really what was once called a 'gown'. Pinned up behind the door was a photograph of the singer Vladimir Vysotsky, a singer repressed by Brezhnev and now an 'unofficial' hero for millions who adore his ballads of booze and boredom. On the wall behind her was a drawing of Oscar Wilde. 'I adore Oscar Wilde.'

'*The Importance of Being Earnest*?'

'*Salome*. To read *Salome* is to die!' Now in her late seventies, Natalya taught English for many years. She laments the lack of what she calls 'finesse'. She was unable ever to remarry after her husband's death. For forty years she rejected would-be suitors for their lack of intellectual finesse. She once rejected a man simply because he mispronounced a word; it was not the mispronunciation to which she objected but the pretension of having used it in the first place.

'We went to the cinema one evening. He wasn't well, he had a cold – 'flu. He apologised to me, he said, "I am *influenced*!" Later he proposed. Naturally I turned him down flat.'

Home-made meat pies and madeira wine, followed by tea, and jam eaten off pretty little silver plates. Natalya did not complain about her cramped room or about the difficulties with the neighbours – a geriatric lady not in her right mind, couples with young and growing families. She feared and detested young people. 'Hostility they have already left behind them. Nowadays they are utterly indifferent. They don't threaten old people. They do not even see them.'

Her room was an island of taste and decorum. Her English was beautifully spoken with emphasised correctness. She was also fluent in French and German and she was presently studying Spanish and Italian on the educational language service of Moscow TV. She was, I believe, a happy woman. Her regret, that the world no longer contained 'finesse', was in fact so large, so fatal, that she had retired from society. It scandalised her. She nodded her head from time to time in silent reproof when yet another example of its gross deficiency occurred to her.

'Have some more jam,' said Natalya. 'I believe the English are still devoted to jam.'

Happiness is a veiled and dangerous concept. Valentin has doubts about its existence. 'Happiness is learnt by example,' he said, 'and there are fewer and fewer people who know what happiness is.'

I wondered about the man in the restaurant who wanted to kill 'blacks'. The Russian language has no such word and speaks of 'negroes' when describing people of African origin. 'Blacks' is a term applied to members of their own southern republics, say the Moslem republics or to Georgians, and of course it can be used as a form of abuse. The writer, Andrei, told me of thousands of 'blacks' who come up to Moscow, of Soviet *gastarbeiter*, migrating from the southern republics.

I made enquiries. Ten thousand 'guest workers' will come to Moscow from other cities in the years 1989–90, according to figures issued by the Moscow City Soviet Executive Committee – the city's unelected, secretive administration. The Moscow City

Soviet is pledged to reduce this number. In fact the numbers have increased year by year since workers cannot be found for the giant Likhachev Plant (Zil) – 'the ecologically negative area' to which Mikhail the driver had introduced me. And the Metro too needs workers which Moscow itself cannot provide. These 'foreign' workers are regarded as transient and temporary. In theory they will return to their 'homelands' at the end of their contractual periods – but in practice that does not happen. Indeed the situation is one any South African would find uncomfortably familiar, for the imported workers are 'temporary sojourners', regrettable necessities, best not discussed. And because these incomers are from the southern republics, they are evidently and immediately alien, they are not 'Russian' and, with Russian nationalism increasing in volume and belligerence, sharpened by the knowledge that ethnic Russians maintain a bare majority throughout the Soviet Union, Muscovites resent the presence in their city of growing numbers of migrant 'blacks'.

Real blacks, Africans in Moscow, are seen as exotic, somewhat troubling creatures, though the more literate and educated classes like to pretend this is not the case. At Moscow University students from Ghana, Uganda and the Francophone countries offered me calm yet compelling evidence of Soviet racialism and the motives behind it. People above the age of fifty were less prone to racialism, while the younger people suffered from its negative symptoms: the belief that black students were given a disproportionate boost by having their fees paid, and free accommodation; that they unfairly took what might otherwise have gone to Russian students; they were arrogant, flashy with their hard currency purchases; and there was Aids, a black disease, an African import – all African students were tested for the disease and in the opinion of many they deserved to be. It was not uncommon for blacks to be taunted in the streets. That the young should be less tolerant than their elders came about, the Ghanaian students suggested, not very plausibly, because the young looked inward and knew nothing but the Soviet Union, while their mothers and fathers at least retained some recollection of the outside world. In the main, the views of many young people were stereotypical, derogatory, derived from bad old movies, full of stock misconceptions and glib caricatures of Africans.

Major trouble sometimes arose when black males were seen with white girls. It was presumed that the girls were inevitably prostitutes. No doubt in some cases they were but the beliefs which underpinned these suppositions were surprising. I was told by otherwise intelligent Muscovites, readers of Pushkin and defenders of freedom, that 'certain white whores' were 'fatally attracted' to black men.

The feeling is there, even in those who deplore it. Andrei, the novelist, told me of the time that he'd been unpleasantly surprised by the strength of his revulsion. Standing outside an hotel waiting for a taxi one night, he watched as a young, teenage girl and her black client joined the queue, still arguing about the price, the girl demanding to know what would happen if she fell pregnant. Eventually they sorted it out between them and the black man left. The girl, deciding perhaps on one last cast of the line, headed back into the hotel, into the swirl of prostitutes around the bar, thickening as evening wore on, one of Moscow's familiar sights, a sub-life which nightly orbits the main hotels, caught within the gravitational pull of foreign comforts – hard currency, cigarettes, champagne, businessmen.

'But she didn't score. No pimp, maybe.'

Most girls are freelancers. Only at the most expensive hotels do you see the pimps, in expensive Italian shoes, smoking Marlboros and earnestly conferring with their girls in the bar as to the trading prospects for the night, while stolid Finnish businessmen stare into the gloom and parties of Americans from Kansas get steadily and noisily drunk.

'Watching her bargaining with her black client I felt disturbed,' Andrei admitted. 'I got a feeling of rage. She was blonde and lovely like a brilliant animal, she was so young, a young Russian girl. And she'd been with the black man. It seemed like a sin. So eventually she comes out again and we're still waiting for a taxi. I looked at her and I had this theory – I was sure she was a country girl, up from a tiny village. I didn't want her to be hurt. She was far from home – and just a child. I could have done something to that black man! Anyway, no taxi came. You know how it is.

Eventually a little bus turned up. I recognised the type, it was the bus that is used to carry the corpse at funerals, but it was late and I didn't mind. Nor did the others standing with me in the snow. We negotiated a price for the round trip and off we set, girl included. It was only after we'd gone some distance that somebody said something about the bus's previous occupation. The girl panicked. I knew then I was right – she was up from the provinces. And she had all the country superstitions. The thought of travelling in a bus which usually carried dead bodies sent her crazy. She became hysterical. She made the driver pull up. We were nowhere and she had no means of getting home. We tried to stop her but she got out of the bus and ran off into the night. I often wonder what happened to her. I also wonder why I felt as I did about the black man. I wished she was back in her village, at home. Where she could live in the way that she understood, where she could marry in the traditional way. And I knew all I wished was rubbish.'

I remember Alya, a big girl with masses of blond hair and long white boots of which she was very proud. She had a soft spot for visitors and conducted the original and most efficient of joint-ventures with foreigners, keeping an eye on them as they strolled through the subway beneath the boulevard. 'Foreign is fun,' said Alya, and she liked to wink when she said it. It was difficult not to wink back, whatever your intentions, since Alya was like that, warm, welcoming and on the game.

'I meet someone, minutes later he's a friend!'

Was foreign fun when it was black? I wondered. Alya considered, touching her nose with the tip of her finger and screwing up her face in concentration.

'Better than some, worse than others. In other words, no difference. Except for Russian people. The trouble with going along with negroes is Russian people – sometimes they get angry. Russian men', Alya pronounced firmly, 'are no fun.'

Her position in the subway beneath the boulevard was perfect. Guests leaving the large hotel across the way would sometimes try to hail a cab and when this failed they would spot the trolley bus stop across the road and dive into the subway. In the subway Alya waited, with her white boots and her pretty silk dress and her warm, sticky smile: a marshmallow spider.

'I talk to them, and that's it . . .' Alya shrugged incredulously as if she had never got used to the ease of it all. 'After a moment we understand one another.'

'Is it a question of price?'

'It's a question of mood. Or maybe of currency. Sometimes it is love alone. We agree then, and I say, "Go to your room and wait." I have many foreign friends. One day I will go to Holland. Yes. And I will not be coming back!'

With her talent for foreign relations, it would be sensible if the Soviet government paid her fare and made an official appointment. She would make the perfect ambassador when people one day move from room to room in the 'European house'.

Many of the girls who work the hotels have their hearts set on meeting a friendly foreigner. Some even hope for marriage – not, as might be thought, because they wish to leave the country but because a foreign marriage of convenience will make them eligible to receive hard currency. Expenses are high; the routine bribe to the doorman in a Moscow hotel is twenty roubles, and sweeteners may be handed out to waiters, policemen and floor ladies. It is, above all, a cheerful, industrious, efficient sorority which, in its professionalism, inventiveness and charm, outperforms and outshines the sour drones on the doors, behind the desks, in the restaurants, whose job it is to provide the big hotels with legitimate goods and services.

Devoted as many of the girls are to foreign affairs, it is their innocence in such matters which is sometimes perturbing. Galia is devoted to a Belgian friend who, she told me in the strictest confidence, was 'very big in personnel'. She spoke of it as if 'personnel' were some fantastic prize given to very few, a land of ultimate content where everyone owned limitless amounts of foreign currency, lipstick was free and Dior dresses hung on trees. Belgium itself had become a place so huge with possibility, so fat with luxury, that Galia could not speak of it without trembling. And the 'bigness' of her friend grew until he filled the sky of her imagination. Galia had applied for permission to visit Belgium.

And when she went (this was so secret she whispered it) she would *not* be coming back.

I hope Belgium is ready.

I wanted to see the source of the brides who fluttered around Red Square in all weathers, and so Nadia took me to the Palace of Weddings. She assured me no one would object. And if they did?

'Well then, we'll simply fill in the forms of marriage. Or we will be important strangers. In the olden days it was customary to invite a few important strangers to your wedding. It gave it a certain grandeur. Such guests were called "wedding generals". Today there are wedding generals in all walks of life. They are a way of putting medals on a poor existence.'

Nadia had the eye of a surgeon and the heart of a sceptic. She denied being a nihilist but she was the purest pessimist I have ever met. Her pessimism was dark and deep and of a refined sort, compounded of fury, grief and despair, forced through the filter of her crushed expectations until it became so terribly clear you forgot how deep it was.

No one objected to us to begin with, they were all too busy filling in the forms, or dozing quietly, or getting married themselves. The Palace of Weddings was a kind of nuptial post office; people came in, were certified and were sent on their way. Large panelled waiting rooms where the chandeliers blazed and walls were mirrors. Sofas accommodated the bridal parties passing through in a steady stream. Someone was practising Mendelssohn's Wedding March on a piano behind closed doors.

We sat down on a sofa. A clerk said, 'What are you sitting there for? This is not your room. Go to another room and wait.' So we went to another room where a number of young couples were filling in forms, seeking permission to marry, and setting dates for their weddings. Many couples must wait a month after putting in the application before they can tie the knot. This is to deter young hotheads from impetuous marriages, which often take place soon after the couple first meet, though some of the boys think better of the plan and never show up for the wedding. In Moscow nearly sixty per cent of brides are under twenty-one; thirty per cent of boys under twenty-two. Notices on the walls urged consultation: *Phone us for tips on traditional marriages, according to old customs*. Nadia went to phone for advice. She came back some time later smiling happily. 'The number is solidly engaged. I can't get through.'

Brides arrived in little explosions of lace; short, round, tall, weeping, in white, pink, lilac. Family and friends bought red carnations at four roubles a bunch in the entrance hall; the door lady looked like a nurse at the end of a long day with troublesome patients; on a big TV set a wedding video played again and again the ceremony the couples would soon go through behind the closed doors, while all around, brothers, mothers, witnesses in red sashes and fathers with cameras continually adjusted their clothing, hair, ties, sashes. Every so often another bride would arrive, on foot, or in an old Zil limousine with fishtails and plenty of chrome, red and pink ribbon stretching from the radiator grill to the windscreen and on its roof two entwined, slightly rusty wedding bells. The big polished doors of a nuptial suite opened wide, the piano struck up the wedding march, and bride and groom moved unsurely down the red carpet towards the wedding officer's desk. Minutes later, the wedding party issued from a side door into an adjoining room where the photographer waited. He sat them down on a sofa, and with the gesture of a parade-ground officer lining up the troops, he had them shot in three minutes flat and on their way out. There were ante-nuptial and post-nuptial waiting rooms, but only the officials knew the difference.

Another of the Palace officials approached us. 'Why are you sitting in this room?'

'Are we not allowed to wait here?'

'Can you see the door?'

'But we were told to wait in this room. Where should we go?'

'Go to another room and wait there.'

Nadia laughed. 'There are two contradictory forces – the expectation of happiness and the impossibility of happiness. Maybe out of the clash comes humour?' The video kept repeating itself; the flower girl slept; the door lady scowled; the wedding march began again. 'Life is caught between dream and coarse reality. Mostly the second.'

We went to another room and waited there. A little bride was examining herself in a great mirror on the wall, a plump moth, a ball of lace, absorbed and exhilarated by the image of her frothy metamorphosis. The sight of so many matrimonial moths hurrying towards the flame repelled Nadia. 'Living together is out of the question – nowhere to live, in the first place. Many are pregnant. They will spend a year or more living with their parents before finding an apartment. Most will divorce in a few years.' Then, very softly, almost to herself and in such a reasonable tone that I thought, just for a moment, she felt she had unduly depressed me, she added, 'And yet I suppose there *is* one thing worse than living in this system . . .' Despite myself, I responded. I should have known better, I knew the signs, but forgetting all I had learnt, I warmed to this unexpectedly optimistic concession.

'What's that?'

'Dying,' said Nadia.

6

Bell and Burial

The girl in the small pink coffin was about ten or eleven. She waited in the laying-out room of the morgue, her face bound in white cloth, hands folded across her breast. Her coffin was open, the lid lay on the floor so that family and friends might bestow a final kiss, in the Russian manner. Her face was a placid mask, that remote, unbearable serenity which is agony for the living. Her mother, accompanied by a family friend, stood beside her, unable to speak.

I had expected the morgue to be empty; it was almost closing time. I felt like an intruder. Then I realised it must be something like this throughout each day. Mourners waiting in the ante-chamber could not help but intrude upon the grief of those taking leave of their loved ones since glass doors led into the laying-out room, where, on a raised black stone slab, the little girl lay in her pink coffin. It was a yellow, peeling building, windows dusty, with all the oppressive seediness of the public kingdom of the bureaucrat, reached by way of a muddy alley running between the morgue and the hospital next door. Chekhov once remarked that the degree of nihilism in Russian literature would be understood by anyone who spent time in the entrance hall of Moscow University. The entrance hall of the Moscow morgue continues that tradition. At the mouth of the alley a small grey van was parked, its back doors open. The driver stood beside his van, smoking and occasionally scrutinising the smoky snow clouds overhead. It was around four on a Saturday afternoon, and bitterly cold. The light was going. A notice beside the front doors curtly informed relatives that collection of bodies took place between nine and four o'clock on weekdays, and between ten and five on Sundays. I felt I should leave but I could not move. I sat on one of the benches in the entrance hall and watched the old janitor, agile, withered, quick as a cricket, busy with his broom around my feet, collecting remnants of cellophane wrapping, bruised carnations, trampled remains of the floral tributes of earlier mourners at other funerals. The old man had big blue eyes, sympathetic eyes, despite his urgent, leathery bustle. It was awkward for him; it was awkward for everyone.

No tenderness; no place for grieving privately, for the cosmetic yet vital consolations of the undertaker's art, no flowers, music, speeches and prayers, no encouragement or displays of human sympathy which help to insulate the heart, to sheath the raw pain of such occasions: all were absent – worse, no one expected them to be there. Dealing with death was, in theory, much the same as dealing with life; it meant putting your hand into the machinery of the system; it meant a queue with a problem at the end of it. The girl had died in the hospital next door, probably without warning because a small bundle of her belongings, wrapped in hospital linen, waited on the floor beside the bier. The man sweeping the floor of the entrance hall was not impatient, he was a model of decorum, but he had a problem. He was anxious to clear up and go home but he could not get into the laying-out room until the family had left.

The girl's mother was paralysed by sorrow, she stooped over the coffin, gazing down at her child, and every now and then she would bend and embrace her. The family friend, tactful and loving, did what she could to comfort her. The father, mercifully, was busy with the arrangements for departure, which seemed complicated. He made many trips between the coffin and the van parked at the end of the alley while the difficulties were discussed. Helping him were two young soldiers, boys in their late teens, clumsy, but well-meaning; nephews perhaps, or it might have been that the father was a military man and the boys came from his unit or regiment. He wore a hat against the bitter cold and whenever he entered the morgue where his daughter lay, he took off his hat. There was nothing sacred about the place, it was not a chapel or church, it was the morgue, yet he took off his hat. When he passed, the janitor stopped sweeping and I stood up. It seemed the least we could do. The young soldiers left their caps in the back of the van.

The man's problems were these. There was a limited amount of space. The coffin of the girl, together with her belongings and those of her parents, had to be accommodated in the back of the small van. Then there was the mud. The metal floor of the van was covered in an inch of mud and the pink coffin, pretty, and padded, would be ruined. Eventually, from somewhere in the morgue, a white sheet was produced and carefully laid down on the floor of the van. All the time the driver looked on, smoking, keeping an eye on the weather and the time. He was not unsympathetic but he was only the driver; he had that look of shamefaced embarrassment which those unwillingly caught up in the intense emotional crises of others sometimes wear. He had offered his van perhaps, or been hired, to bring the dead girl home and he was anxious to get on the road. It was going to be a long ride, the number plates on the van showed that it came from Leningrad.

At last arrangements were complete. With the father directing operations, the two young soldiers went into the room where the girl lay. The friend of the family took the mother in her arms and gently turned her away while the soldiers placed the lid on the coffin; then with the aching delicacy that looks like clumsiness but comes of quivering gentleness, they carried the small coffin through the swing-doors with a solemn grandeur, like an honour guard, and the janitor and I stiffened as they passed, and they slid it into the back of the van.

It was a very narrow fit. The white sheet had a tendency to ride on the metal ribs of the floor and had to be smoothed out carefully. The bundle in the hospital sheet and other bits and pieces were placed around the coffin – the state of the roads out of Moscow is not good and unless the coffin was decently wedged it was likely to bounce. At last it was time to go. The two soldiers climbed into the back of the van and perched awkwardly on the bundles of possessions and the door was closed. The friend of the family tried to persuade the parents to eat something before leaving Moscow.

'Our friends would feel *so* hurt if you didn't stop at their place. They're expecting you. It's a long way to go. Please, at least let us give you some hot food.'

I cannot say for certain but I think the plea fell on deaf ears. Mother and father squeezed into the cab beside the driver, and the funeral procession rolled out of the alley just as the last light faded. On the hospital wall opposite the morgue entrance, mourners turned vandals had scribbled the names of Western heavy-metal rock groups; Slade and Genesis were specially cherished.

I watched as the janitor finished the last of his sweeping in the room where the little girl had lain. It was a tiled circular chamber; the black stone slab at its centre looked like an altar. The tiles around the room were black and old. In two niches in the wall stood small funerary statues, weeping women, personifications of grief, relics perhaps from pre-Revolutionary times, faintly Grecian, distantly artistic, vaguely religious. For some reason a string of coloured paper leaves hung from a section of the ceiling and rustled in the breeze whenever the big glass door opened. The nimble sweeper stuck his broom into nooks and corners, quick as a chameleon; he smiled at me in a friendly, imploring way. I took the hint and left. It had been a long day.

In a sense one might say that many people struggling for change are haunted by the knowledge that the history of modern Russia, rather like *Hamlet*, is haunted by the commission of a crime. The arch-criminal was Stalin. The world which people inhabit was made by him, more so than by anybody else; the crime involved was murder and murder makes ghosts, guilt, victims. There is now no crime, no matter how heinous, for which Stalin cannot be blamed. The ghosts are crying loudly for revenge, the unnamed millions do not rest easily in their graves.

As Stalin bears a growing burden of guilt, Lenin enjoys a disproportionate load of praise, and the queues to his tomb lengthen. In fact there is a queue for the queue. It is situated about a quarter of a mile from the Lenin Mausoleum itself and begins in the gardens beside the Kremlin wall; maybe sixty or seventy people are waiting to join the real queue which snakes ahead, up through the gardens and round the corner, across the cobbles of Red Square and then makes a ninety degree turn into the Mausoleum itself. After fifteen or twenty minutes in the queue for the queue, batches of ten or twenty are allowed (that is to say, are waved on peremptorily by a policeman) to join the real queue. We shuffle forward obediently, silently, watched every ten metres or so by a militia man muttering into his walkie-talkie.

What can be said of the way the policemen watch the queue? There was a revolution here once, or twice (if you count February 1918 as well as the Glorious October Revolution), and the authorities have been determined ever since that nothing of the sort should happen again. Crowds are to be watched, marshalled, scrutinised, patrolled, infiltrated, disciplined, despised and, where necessary, dispersed.

In response, people in crowds display a kind of inflamed docility, a furious meekness which characterises everyone from men in the vodka queue to the delegates to the Supreme Soviet. Indeed it is a quality especially to be observed among the members of that august body, it is a fine example of what Victor the waiter calls 'the art of looking away'. For each of those faces is guarded and docile, conscious they are on show; the features take on the consistency of buttermilk; enquiring glances from strangers slide off the closed countenances; the eyes, though open, turn inwards. When, for instance, Mr Gorbachev speaks, flanked by the Politburo, the faces become a field of pallid sunflowers inclining in unison towards the distant source of warmth; however, the *eyes* do not stray but stare fixedly ahead. Applause patters obediently. Each face must find its strategy for giving nothing away. Among the most original performers in this facial theatre was Mr Kosygin. His face, in official repose, became soft, feminine, almost girlish, there was a kind of simper to the lips, a flutter to the eyelashes, which contrasted strangely with the stony face he gave himself on diplomatic occasions.

Ordinary Russians carry this talent into their private lives. Some of the most inspiring, heroic people I know in Moscow have carried this disdainful obedience to great heights. It is not to be confused with anger, or discontent, as is felt and expressed in Western societies towards political ineptitude or injustice. This feeling goes far beyond anger. It expresses itself in cold contempt for the present political authorities, or in icy indifference to talk of reform; worst is when it no longer trusts itself to use words at all, having fallen so far into bitter disenchantment that it cannot talk of such things, and becomes a statement of pauses, silences, shrugs, grimaces and references so distant from, and oblique to, the subject in question that it sounds, or at least *looks*, like a Beckett play, black despair rattling with melancholy laughter, like gravel on a coffin lid.

No one speaks in the queue for Lenin's tomb except the little boy in front of me, who keeps asking his mother, 'Why have we been waiting here for so long?' Several people quietly admire the prophetic nature of his question.

After half an hour's progress at the slow shuffle, we draw abreast of the Tomb of the Unknown Soldier. A pillar of flame dances upwards as if it were a fiery spring; the snowflakes seem drawn towards the column of fire like moths, they fling themselves into it and are consumed. Another fifteen minutes sees us into the square itself. The cobbles of Red Square, as Ivan the hunchback once showed me, recall the curvature of the earth. Away on our left is the eerily opulent façade of the Universal State Store, GUM; ahead are the onion-mad domes of St Basil's Cathedral; and on our right the cobbles flow on until they are checked by the long defensive wall of the Kremlin itself. In this weather, and in this light, we look like the queue for a soup kitchen as we shuffle forward, occasionally stamping our feet and blowing on our hands. Painted on the cobbles is a long white line and a policeman walks up and down this line making sure that people do not stray the couple of inches that carries them across its surface. You may not cross this line, you may not even set foot on it. Everything is run on such lines, it is the look of the thing that counts; life goes on elsewhere, out of sight, out of mind; that is where the real business gets done, of which nobody speaks, of which nothing appears; in public be sure only that you do not step out of line, or on the line.

The queue makes a right turn as it approaches the mouth of the tomb, still following the white line. The Mausoleum is really a bunker, solid, sturdy, originally built of oak in 1924 but now of red and black granite. This is where the brides come to lay their red carnations. On either side of the doorway two sentries, chosen for their height, stand with fixed bayonets.

A flight of steps into the hushed and holy darkness, even more guards are crammed into this small space; we are moving all the time, in single file, past the illuminated glass coffin where the supreme architect of the first socialist state lies in dark suit and tie, as pale and chalky as the meringues in the Exhibition of Economic Achievements, looking as if he, too, has been constructed from plaster of Paris. Our shadows are cast on the further wall by the light from the glass coffin and move in much the same way as Plato, in *The Republic*, imagined the shadows of imprisoned men moving on the wall of the cave, phantoms cast by the firelight, shadows of illusion. This is the holy of holies, the tabernacle created by the same impulse which moved the ancient Egyptians to eviscerate and then mummify their pharoahs; the faith which displays the miraculously preserved body of Saint Vincent de Paul in a glass-and-silver casket in a Paris church; it is a very human, stubborn, perverse thing to do and it is done for age-old childlike reasons, to give the fierce pleasure of preserving something against the wreck of time. It is responsible for that curious shiver of guilty joy we feel when the body of a prehistoric mammoth rears entire in a wall of ice, or in the Arctic a party of frozen explorers are uncovered, or an Iron Age man, strangled and buried in a peat bog, is hauled to the surface and confronts us. It is the impulse behind graveyards, memorials, gardens of remembrance, it is a grim little game we play against time, despite reason's warning cough or fierce whisper that it cannot be true, all succumb to it at one time or another – 'But yes, if you just close your eyes, just narrow them a bit, then it almost *might* be true!' And the little man in the dark suit with the chalky face and the pointy beard might be not dead but only asleep . . . And so it is for religious reasons that we have come here, waiting our turn patiently to file past the miraculously preserved body of the saint. We are pilgrims in anoraks.

The glass coffin on its plinth, this cube of controlled air, the carefully restored masterpiece of the Revolution, the honour guards motionless, bayonets fixed. Then, without warning, the intense effort required, if things are to seem eternal, is betrayed, when a fresh guard detail come goose-stepping into the sanctuary and we are hurried on, for no one may pause or look back.

When Stalin died in 1953 his body was mummified and laid beside that of Lenin. No one mentions that. He was denounced by Krushchev in 1956, and in 1961 his body was removed. Those who saw them both here will describe how they lay side by side, two terrifying little men. Presumably this building was known as the Lenin–Stalin Mausoleum. When the Soviet leaders take their places on the roof of the Mausoleum to celebrate the anniversary of the October Revolution, it is an assertion that, by merely standing on this spot, they are establishing a kind of apostolic succession.

Then to the necropolis, the honoured graves, the Garden of Remembrance which lies behind the Lenin Mausoleum. A strange democracy of the dead prevails. You may not approach the sacred place without first passing through the Mausoleum. Buried in the Kremlin wall are Party leaders, astronauts, pilots, honoured foreigners, murderers, apparatchiks, heroes and charlatans, their resting places marked by small black plaques. A line of blue spruce trees add further to the sense of the funereal occasion. Directly opposite the black plaques in the wall are a series of grave-like monuments, a miniature Valley of the Kings, rows of marble headstones crowned by a collection of remarkably unrepresentational carved heads of the country's leaders. Here, for instance, is a very youthful Chernenko, an extremely avuncular Andropov; idealised and noble – for these are the tombs of the Soviet pharaohs. Stalin is here, rejoicing in a clean-cut jaw and almost youthful air. There is every indication that this little gathering of the good and the bad and the monstrous will increasingly constitute a problem, simply by its presence. The skeletons wait in the cupboards. Some ought never to have been buried here. And how many others, who perhaps deserve a place, are scattered elsewhere? Small wonder that schoolchildren have stopped reading history for the past year, when history moves in such convulsive stages, when it can be here one day and gone the next. Those who wish to continue the lesson do not need to wait for the revised texts, they can, if they wish, go and read the graveyards.

I was haunted by the photographs of Chekhov's funeral in 1904. Photographs lodged in his small house on Sadovaya-Kudrinskaya Street, dwarfed by tower blocks, marshmallow pink among the mastodons. Chekhov's funeral cortège moving down Kuznetsky Lane, crowded with ghostly faces turning to watch the hearse go by, faces you cannot find in Moscow any longer: perfectly ordinary, early-twentieth-century faces; men in hats, dark eyes, the bourgeosie; thin faces, watch-chains, canes, high collars, boots. The horses drawing Chekhov's hearse wore white coverings with eye-holes cut into the fabric, phantom horses with black eyes, moving through crowds of the exterminated classes.

Viktoria, a librarian and translator, ponders the question of where they went, those faces. Stalin, she says, managed to create a generation of people who were not people, and she recalls a remark of Dostoevsky's, that it took two generations to destroy a nation. In the Soviet Union there have been three generations since Chekhov, more than time enough to do away with the refinements of centuries. To recapture the human virtues of dignity and spirituality is almost impossible, she thinks, because there is nothing to build on, for Stalin contrived to kill not only people, he managed to kill the soil in which this civilisation once took root.

Viktoria is, like Hamlet, desperate with imagination, full of a restless impatience to see the latest reforms and growing freedoms preserved and extended, but her hopes are eaten into by a corrosive fear that the thaw may end abruptly. Her overwhelming desire to support the new changes is taking its toll, exhausting time and energies which would otherwise go into her work. She talks feelingly of the survivors of Stalin's camps and she quotes an eighty-two-year-old who 'managed to survive' or, as he told her, 'contrived to avoid the many attempts made to kill him'. She has considered, and rejected, the option of emigration, though she admits being tempted to visit America – but only 'for a rest'. America, she says wistfully, must be so peaceful.

Recalling Stalin's death in 1953, when she was five, she remembers a frenzied, ugly grief in the centre of Moscow, the sky lit up with an enormous picture of the dead dictator, 'a portrait of Stalin flying in the air', people trampled by the hysterical crowds, a young boy she knew crushed in the tumult. She felt ill, she ran a temperature and her grandmother sat by her bedside and said to her, 'People shouldn't be glad when a person dies but it is very good that he died. Maybe, *maybe*, there won't be so many tragedies.' Her grandmother allowed herself another crumb of comfort after Krushchev's denunciatory speech of Stalin in 1956. 'Now we have some chance.' Her grandfather, an architect who enjoyed Stalin's esteem, took no chances even so and in the corner of his study he always kept a small trunk. She used to play on it, she remembers. It was only much later that she realised that the trunk held her grandfather's things, ready for the late-night knock on the door.

Viktoria admits that most people do not care either way about reform and she cites the battle to change the name of the district where she works. It is called Zhdanov and commemorates Stalin's most notorious 'cultural commissar'. Of the 650 people polled at her place of work, 100 are against the change, about 200 wish to see it revert to its pre-Stalinist name and two think it should be called after Stalin. The rest are coldly indifferent and do not even wish to hear the subject raised. People in their early twenties and below that age neither know nor care about Stalin; this indifference is summed up by one of her young colleagues, a girl of twenty-four, who turned beautiful grey eyes on Viktoria and demanded, 'Why should I worry? It was before my time!'

Many of the campaigners for reform are women, Viktoria suggests, simply because women will not be deterred. It can be hard on the family. 'My husband is thinking of joining a group called "Husbands Against Perestroika". I am a feminist, which is to say I am a Russian woman. If a feminist from the West came here and lived as a Russian woman for two weeks, there would be no trace of feminism left in her.'

Her formidable faith in the need for a more open society is

accompanied by a profound scepticism of the motives behind recent political reforms. When she talks of perestroika she handles the word as if she wielded a pair of tweezers, delicately, gingerly, keeping it at arm's length and averting her nose.

'It's reminiscent of Lenin's New Economic Policy in the twenties. Boris Pasternak wrote one line which is worth volumes on this subject. He wrote that the policy of NEP was "a colossal manifestation of political hypocrisy". We're told we must build a new economic policy. But on *what* must we build? How do you make bricks without straw? You've been in our shops. You've seen how bad it is. And it is not getting better, it is getting worse.'

On street corners the hawkers are busy, appearing from nowhere, mobbed by crowds of exhilarated shoppers who moments before had been mere passers-by. Egyptian oranges sold from an open truck, spilling from cardboard boxes, the colour wild, like stolen gold. On the next corner, piles of crates build an outdoor beer hall, eager customers, in the Moscow dusk, stand knocking back the big bottles in the pelting snow.

Everybody is encouraged to remember Stalin; as a hero he was inescapable, as a monster he is more necessary than ever. 'Anybody can imagine bad things,' said Victor the waiter contemptuously, 'but name me a place where the worst you can imagine always comes true. Was it Tolstoy? – yes, I think it was Tolstoy – who said, "Imagine Genghis Khan with a telephone!" It happened! And we got Stalin.'

Stalin was a short man, five foot two inches, a failed poet in elevated shoes. A jailed seminarian, he spent five years in a theology college in the Georgian city of Tiflis, before being thrown out for reading the wrong sorts of books. Later he robbed banks in the Caucasus to raise money to fund his political programme. The transformation of Stalin into the semi-divine being whose people rioted upon news of his death on 5 March 1953 was guided by his praise-singers. His poets compared him to spring sunshine. For comparable paeans of praise today you would have to go to the court of President Ceausescu of Romania, 'the Great Conducator', 'the Danube of Thought'. Stalin's court painters were warned to favour his right profile and Shurpin and Gerasimov, in their devotional portraits, show him mourning a comrade-at-arms or contemplating the great sweep of the Russian steppe, adopting a prayerful, contemplative pose. The songs he encouraged were dreadful, with lines like, 'Hello, country of heroes, country of dreams, country of scientists' – but everyone sang them.

Poetry was something Stalin caught, like an infection, rather young. He survived the attack, but real poets were not so fortunate. Rulers, it seemed, were permitted to dabble. It is interesting to recall that Andropov while head of the KGB was an amateur poet; one wonders if he reflected on the fate of many great Russian poets. Gumilev was executed; Blok died mysteriously (his admirers say he died 'of death'); Esenin and Mayakovsky killed themeselves; Mandelstam died in a prison camp; Pasternak was hounded until his death; Tsvetaeva hanged herself; Akhmatova, persecuted by the ineffable Zhdanov as the 'harlot nun', was unable to publish; Brodsky was forced into exile.

Among Stalin's more unlikely liquidations was the Esperanto Society which was, as they say, 'disrupted' in 1938. It has just been rehabilitated. For their part, Stalin and his supporters remain members of the Communist Party, to which, being eternal rather like the Church Universal, members may continue to belong after death; moreover, membership may be restored to the excommunicated after they have gone to the Great Politburo in the sky. This has happened to many of Stalin's victims. Some people continue to call for the dictator's expulsion from the Party, but this has not been achieved. No one has been expelled from the Party after death. 'If we began,' asked an official Party historian, 'where would we stop?'

Fevered anticipation tinged with fear among Moscow intellectuals is accompanied by the daunting realisation, just as it was in *Hamlet*, that corruption is so overwhelming that perhaps nothing can cure it. So they have seized on a tangible issue; underlying crimes must be addressed, reparation must be offered to those whose lives were 'disrupted', often fatally, and the ancestors appeased – and that is why the victims of Stalin are so important, and why there are the demands that they be remembered. What makes this such a radical demand is that, until recently, memory has been the mechanical department of state. The 'memory' of the State was like the mind of God: if it forgot you for a moment you disappeared forever.

Memory, thus, is reparation, memory is the weapon. A group called 'Memorial' has dedicated itself to rehabilitating the victims of the camps. The numbers of those repressed, imprisoned, purged, deported and murdered by Stalin, when taken together, run into tens of millions, according to the admittedly conservative estimates of the Soviet historian Roy Medvedev, who dates the first wave of mass repressions from 1927–28 when Stalin turned in fury on the followers of Trotsky and Zinoviev. Writing in *Moscow News*, Medvedev pointed out that repression started earlier than anyone suspected and simply went into top gear with the dispossession of the kulaks and the famine of 1933 in the southern Ukraine. The terror reached its height after the assassination of Kirov in 1934, following through to the prodigious killing year of 1937. None of this will come as a surprise to readers of Robert Conquest's seminal study *The Great Terror*. Yet even before 1937, which many in the West date as the beginning of the 'Great Terror', Stalin had victimised at least 17 to 18 million people, and of those some 10 million had either died or had been murdered. And killings and purges continued to the end, right through to the final period of 1947–53. It was a devastation unparalleled in human history.

But getting the facts is another thing. The very notion of a 'fact' has been much abused. When Stalinists, and the Party, decided to make a non-person of you, you stayed a non-person for good. The archives of the secret police, the Cheka and the NKVD, which are known to exist, have still not been released to the investigators, and though many victims of Stalin's purges have been declared 'persons' again, even their rehabilitation papers remain classified. Those who survived the deportation points and the camps are now being interviewed and memories collected. It is very late in the day. No records exist, there are no letters from the camps, no caches of photographs, there is none of the grainy film footage we associate with the Jewish Holocaust, there is just silence and, occasionally, a field full of skeletons.

Ghosts of Stalin's victims are coming out of concealment, helped into the light by careful excavation, the farmer's plough, soil erosion. Some of the killing fields have been excavated by archaeologists mounting professional digs, analysing the material, drawing conclusions and preparing reports, as if investigating the grave-pits of a remote and murderous alien culture. *Literatura i Lastatstva* has printed reports of the excavations near Kuropaty, not far from Minsk. At this place, in a forest, day after day groups of the condemned were shot by special detachments of the NKVD. The sound of gunfire reached the peasants working in the fields and became a familiar accompaniment through the period from 1937 to 1939. Victims were gagged and blindfolded and killed with a rifle shot; economies were practised, orders were to kill two with one bullet. Squads of NKVD officers worked in shifts finishing at about eleven o'clock at night and then made their way to the village dance. Over 100,000 people were shot in this area in the late thirties and the social classes varied, according to the belongings found buried with the executed. Indeed the classes were segregated. Excavations revealed peasant shoes and bits of rough tableware in some graves. In others medicines were found, spectacles, even a monocle and women's fancy gloves. No doubt some of those who watched Chekhov's funeral, and attended his plays, ended in these mass graves.

To meet some of the survivors is to be struck by their cheerfulness and their terrifying modesty. I sat in the Tchaikovsky Hall listening to the first performance of a requiem composed in honour of these little old people who seemed rather abashed at all the fuss, sweet-tempered and slightly restless. Three choirs, a symphony orchestra and a speech from the poet Yevtushenko provided an air of solemnity entirely lacking among the audience, who gave the impression of being out on a picnic and determined not to let gloomy memories spoil their fun.

'Have a cookie,' whispered the elderly lady sitting beside me, fourteen years in a camp, no survivors among her family, passing me a brown paper bag full of honey cookies. 'You look a bit peckish. And it's going to be a long evening. Go on, help yourself, and pass them down the row.'

Not pain or anguish, but serene good spirits, a shining joy in having attained an unexpected status, being alive and well and eating cookies.

The only sharp note came from someone too young to have known the Stalin years and angry on the victims' behalfs. Looking at Yevtushenko as he spoke eloquently of the need to remember Stalin's crimes, Nadia said bitterly in the darkness, 'Of course, he is the sort of poet doomed to survive under any government.'

Others remember Stalin for their own reasons, and the warmth of their memories reflects the near-hysterical adoration once felt for him by millions of Soviet people. The intensity of this affection lingers here and there and is best summed up by an anonymous correspondent to a Moscow newspaper, who writes, 'We believed in Comrade Stalin, and our life was good. Comrade Stalin was concerned about people, and the shops were full.'

It seems to be, or to become, the fate of Russian rulers to resemble unpromising earlier models. Stalin was said to have an obsession with Ivan the Terrible. If, in the minds of his conservative opponents, Mr Gorbachev is to be compared with anyone it might be with the 'False Tsar' Dmitry (1580–1606). What infuriated Muscovites was Dmitry's open encouragement of Western European behaviour, the scepticism he showed towards religious beliefs and the frivolous Western indulgences of his wife. This 'false' Dmitry was brutally murdered by his subjects and his remains fired from a cannon in Red Square.

Only once did I beat Valentin at his own sad, elegant game of 'What could be worse?' For there is, I discovered, something worse than either living or dying in Moscow, and that is growing old alone. Since most families find room for aged relatives, the tragedy is confined to little-known institutions which few people care to visit.

The floor lady in the Old Age Home was dozing, and gently snoring, a study in audible contentment. The slogan in the window of the Meeting Room, set aside (as it must be in all such places) for Party members among the staff, advised, 'The workers and the intellectuals must be one and the same!' It sounded vaguely like Lenin. No one was paying any attention. The Meeting Room was empty. So were the corridors of the Home, a musty nine-storey building tucked away behind new and rather desirable blocks of flats for the rising technocrats of the University. The inmates were finishing lunch; some were leaving the dining-room in twos and threes, on sticks and in walking frames and wheelchairs. Silence and the aroma of cabbage. The dining-room boasted the giant display cabinet, that cherished item of furniture in polite households called 'a wall'. There was little in or on the wall but its presence signified a certain pretension, at least among the designers of the home back in the sixties, which nothing in its present manifestation attempted to live up to anymore. Someone had been painting the corridors olive-green, but had stopped.

The smell of new paint faded as I climbed the stairs. On the lower floors were the walking elderly, still able to leave their rooms and venture down to the dining-room. When they were not at meals, they wandered the long, dim corridors or stood in anxious attitudes in odd corners of the building as if waiting for a bus which never came. The home gave them a roof over their heads, meals were provided, and signs on a couple of the doors read *Doctor*, though no medical staff were to be seen, just a couple of young nurse companions on the lower floors. No human touch intruded, not a book, a rug, a radio, and no visitors. These were forgotten people. The ammoniac silence of the corridors, disturbed only by the shuffle of bedroom slippers or the percussive beat of the walking-frame.

It got worse as I climbed higher. On the sixth and seventh floors lay the bed-ridden, the senile, the incontinent. The top two floors concealed the terminally ill, emaciated scraps of flesh and bone who seemed too small even for their small beds – sometimes not enough remained to do more than crease the sheet that covered them – patient morsels, a lingering reminder that even at death's door one could expect to wait, for each person is his own queue.

The truly terrible thing is to be put on the wrong floor. 'That was the worst for a friend of mine,' says Viktoria, as we walked the corridors. 'He had to come here because his family wouldn't take him in and he had lost his flat, been cheated out of it. But they put him on one of the top floors. When I came to visit him he was nearly mad. It took a lot of organisation to get him down to a lower floor. And a large bribe. But I couldn't leave him up there. He was all right, you see. Simply old.'

'You wish to see a Beckett play because you believe Beckett goes to the heart of the matter? I've got good news.' Viktoria handed me a couple of tickets for *Waiting for Godot*.

It was a disconcerting evening. The actors were slim, agile as acrobats, stylish pierrots. It was all very elegant and poetic. I began to feel terribly uneasy. The tramps dressed with more style than most people on the Moscow streets and Beckett's despair turned into shapely choreography.

'It was too beautiful,' I told Viktoria later.

'Beautiful? Ah, you don't mean beautiful.' Viktoria was amused. 'You see, when you put Beckett into the Soviet context he becomes quite romantic.' She thought for a moment. 'Beckett is the Soviet Byron!'

Rumour abounds in political matters, as in all else, and speeds abroad. On the run-up to elections meetings were held on shop-floors, earnest and interminable. The best meetings, as with everything in Moscow, were those which never took place. Boris Yeltsin was expected daily in several corners of the city. Rumour confirmed his imminent arrival. People began to assemble. And police. And the curious, anxious to know why people were assembling: was it for Finnish shoes? Or Hungarian chickens? They came with carnations, with their lame and halt, as if to

Lourdes. The traffic choked up; the floor ladies from surrounding apartment blocks leaned from their windows. I was caught up in one such mass expectation and was unable to leave the area. The militia man on the corner closed the only access road. And when Yeltsin failed to appear we swallowed our disappointment, or surmised darkly that 'they' had forbidden it. The militia man reluctantly opened the road.

'I'm disappointed,' he confessed, 'I would have liked to talk to him about crime. Crimes of violence are increasing in Moscow. In a week there may be as many as four murders. It's almost as bad as New York.'

'Not quite.'

'There were five rapes and fifty-one burglaries last week.'

'Chicken feed – if you're thinking of New York.'

'Twenty-four cars stolen, sixty-one delinquents arrested.'

'Small beer.'

That gave him an idea. 'Six thousand drunks picked up! How about that? Not bad, hey? Do they have that in New York?'

I said I thought that knocked New York cold.

If Beckett is Byronic in the Soviet Union, it is not surprising that graveyards should be friendly places. They allow the eye to rest, and the dead do not tell lies, though their relatives sometimes do that for them. Something like the Praga principle also operates in the graveyards. I tried to visit the Novodevichy Cemetery where Anton Chekhov is buried. Entry was refused, however, because the place was 'full'. I was with a group of writers and on receiving our guide's request that he admit us, the director of the cemetery sent an unexpected response.

'You have writers out there. I have many readers in here. Good day!'

I went to the Vagankovskoye Cemetery instead. The beautiful little church at the gate was crowded with icons, and in the porch a casket wrapped in red cloth, into which the coffin was placed before burial, leaned against the wall, a practical idea, like a reusable rocket launcher. The church was real and functioning; people took off their hats, knelt and crossed themselves. On the left of the door was a vivid painting of Christ raising the dead child of the Roman centurion; altogether it was a place noisy with the hope of an afterlife.

Just inside the cemetery gates was the tomb of Vladimir Vysotsky. Vysotsky, who died in 1980, is in the process of being canonised, he is becoming a secular saint. A little booth did a brisk trade in photographs of his tomb, a large monument cast in bronze depicting the singer emerging from a kind of tube, swathed in his winding sheet. The resurrectional symbolism is unmistakable. Reborn, much as the centurion's dead child sits up, dead white and startled, in the painting in the church opposite, or Lazarus staggers from his sepulchre, his winding sheet unravelling like an onion, Vysotsky arises from rumpled cerements. He has forced a bare shoulder clear and stares out at the world, the human butterfly emerging from its cocoon. Framing his head is his guitar, a curvacious halo, and then directly behind and above the guitar, the heads of two horses modelled by somebody fascinated by the horses on the Parthenon – related perhaps to something he sang or something he said or quite possibly, given the lush rhetoric of gesture in this country, simply to something the sculptor happened to like – parallel, triangular heads with flared nostrils, horses at full tilt, chariot horses, war horses. And all around the grave, which has been fenced in, stand the solemn admirers, thirty, forty, fifty of them maybe, and one by one they slip inside the enclosure and lay more red carnations on the grave which is already piled high with flowers. At times like this it is almost possible to feel some sympathy with the Bolsheviks who attempted the mad, improbable, foolish project of rooting out the religious instincts of the Russian people. Beside this, official efforts to portray Stalin as a democrat and kindly family man seem a minor delusion.

Behind this figurehead, which sat as it were on the prow of the cemetery in much the way that a ship's masthead once adorned the bows of a ship, lay the graveyard itself, a peaceful, snowy, friendly place, clean and well-swept and chattering away, as cemeteries will, like a talking book. Before the Revolution, when Moscow was a cosmopolitan city, the Greek Sotiriadis family lay down with the Pavlovs, each enclosed in a little cage built of wood or wire, with a bench on which the family could rest, having performed the graveside courtesies. You can still see the little broom of birch twigs which was used to sweep away the snow. The more devout families liked to put up one of these little houses on the estates of the departed, they look rather like summer-houses or birdcages. The modern graves are functional, in marble or granite, bearing a photograph of the departed. Generals in all their ribbons, their faces peer out at you like baby ghosts; fading men in stiff suits and still more medals; carved granite heads with angry stares, cousins of Ozymandias, King of Kings – 'Look on my works, ye Mighty, and despair!' Except you do not despair, you can barely read their names.

On another visit I was allowed to spend an afternoon at the Novodevichy Cemetery; that which was 'full' became 'empty' upon the whim of the invisible director who exercises the prerogative cherished beyond riches: power without responsibility. Here are buried the great and notorious of old Russian society and new Soviet power. Chekhov's modest grave is planted with a small cherry tree. Also buried there is Nadezhda Stalin, the Kremlin mountaineer's first wife. A white marble swan, its neck curving gracefully in an undulating line, the very contour of gentle grief, commemorates a great ballerina. A huge, bald general, hero of the Soviet armoured divisions, emerges from a block of solid marble which peels away from his body like molten lava; head first he bursts into the world like brutal pupa, a faraway look in his eyes and all his medals on his chest; and at the foot of his metamorphic column is a small green tank like a child's toy on which someone has left red tulips and carnations. Over there, in the quarter of the Party big-shots, an important man lifts a telephone to his ear. Some frugal member of the great man's family has taken precautions against the winter and wrapped him in plastic sheeting tied with tape so he looks like a hostage phoning the police. Nikita Krushchev's grave is most unexpected of all, made of interlocking blocks of black and white marble. The monument was sculpted by Ernst Neivestny whom Krushchev once censured in the sixties for his modernist tendencies. The artist's mischievous, macabre riposte is wonderful: on the block is a severed head; Nikita's broad, black marble, peasant head – the head, metaphorically at least, Nikita lost when deposed in a Kremlin coup.

And where else in Moscow may the eye rest? Where is there relief from the bruising assault on the optic nerves, brought about by a never-ending succession of violent images? Well, there is the ballet – not the Bolshoi, overpriced and uncomfortable – but the view from below stairs, from the kitchen where art is cooked.

High above a courtyard in a jumble of once-elegant pre-Revolutionary buildings, the Moscow Ballet were rehearsing in an old studio. The dancing master had very tiny feet, the tiniest I had ever seen on a man. His relationship with his young and enthusiastic dancers at the bar was that of a polite yet merciless lash, a talking whip. A line of Christmas trees cut from cardboard were slung from the ceiling, behind them a string of angels with unexpectedly Chinese eyes. On an out-of-tune piano the accompanist played American popular melodies, ranging from 'Dancing in the Dark' to 'Over the Rainbow'. The dancing master whips up his ingredients. 'Here we prepare our dishes made of blood and sweat.' Exercise and ambition leaving an individual contour upon each dancer, fingerprints of time, impressed like a potter's prints in clay; discipline has drawn the line of the dancers' bodies, but it has also set them free.

'Here we go again, falling in love with love!' Russian dancers answering to French directions and moving to American music submit themselves to habitual tortures, the usual impossible stringencies. Ballet is a form of human dressage, the dancers are put through their paces like graceful horses. The ultimate urge is to defy gravity altogether and, where that is not possible, to despise it.

Viktoria again talks of her need to rest. Her American friend has written to her with an invitation: 'Come to America, and relax for a while.' Instead we go to Gorky Park to join a protest meeting. 'Gorky Park,' Viktoria explained, 'is called a Park of Culture and Rest. Moscow has Parks of Culture, Palaces of Culture and

Ministers of Culture. The only thing it lacks is, quite simply, culture.' The occasion of the protest, organised by the Memorial Society, was the thirty-sixth anniversary of Stalin's death. There was a crowd of perhaps about two thousand, and television cameras from all the international networks surrounded the speakers' platform. An air of organised chaos, not one meeting but several, with banners and slogans reading: 'No more victims, no more gunmen.' Two men in the crowd began arguing about Stalin and a small group formed around them. The big man was saying, 'The only programme you have is the analysis of Stalin and his crimes – that is not a programme. That is not enough to build a case on.'

The poet Yevtushenko spoke first and was greeted with enthusiastic applause though it took some ten minutes before the sound system operated at a level which allowed at least some of the crowd closest to him to hear what he was saying. At no point could he be seen because he was entirely surrounded by the cameramen from the Western television networks. There followed one minute of silence in memory of the victims. I once heard the poet Vosnezhensky deplore this custom. 'I tell my students we have had enough of silence. Instead, I told them, we'll have a minute's noise. Shout your heads off!' Looking around at the faces in the crowd during the minute of silence I saw that most were middle-aged or elderly, there were few young people, no workers. Those out in the giant factories and the acres of desolate housing estates do not sit talking excitedly in their kitchens of the crimes of Stalin. The day's shopping has exhausted them, or vodka has dulled them, and the system has utterly disenchanted and alienated them. They will not see pictures of the Memorial demonstration on their televisions; those pictures are for export only, they will amuse or intrigue foreign television viewers for a few minutes. And even if these pictures were shown on Moscow television, there is no guarantee that they would evoke much interest. On the contrary, the scepticism of the average Moscow television viewer is so profound about the items of news that are shown to him that he probably would have difficulty believing in it. A Russian expression says, 'The best lie is the truth.' Such gatherings really are unique events in Moscow but that is not in itself enough to exhilarate the average citizen.

Since there is almost no tradition of speaking for oneself in the Soviet Union, and none at all of the notion of individual responsibility, it is probably not surprising that the new freedoms seem always to be articulated not by individuals but by groups, official and unofficial, with names like the Moscow Popular Front, Memorial, Memory (*Pamyat*), the Democratic Perestroika Club; a bewildering plethora of guilds and sodalities ranging from body-builders to ecologists. The Stalinists are just another contending group yet the language they use is as chilling now as it was then, compounded of clichés, threats and the concrete-collared prose so beloved of tyrants. Thus the present-day supporters of perestroika, that is to say the denigrators of Stalin, are called by a writer to the *Moscow News*, '. . . Sceptics and whiners, direct and indirect descendants of the classes defeated by the Revolution, . . . trying to use the serious economic difficulties today to undermine the trust of the masses in the country's great historic past.'

More potent and disturbing are groups on the nationalist right. I was met at the offices of the magazine *Our Contemporary*, a severely 'patriotic Russian' periodical, by a small burly man wearing a black beret tilted ominously over his right ear. Similar individuals are to be found at the headquartes of the militant nationalist organisation called *Pamyat*, along with framed items of Nazi regalia which are kept, they will tell you politely – and what other word would do? – simply as 'mementoes'. Their creed is nationalism merging with chauvinism and reaching into crypto-fascism, with strong anti-Semitic tendencies here called, for convenience, 'anti-Zionism'. Such organisations as *Pamyat* and *Our Contemporary* support the growing nationalist movements in the Baltic republics of Estonia, Lithuania and Latvia, as well as the struggle for the independence in Armenia (for much the same reason as white right-wing groups in South Africa support separate 'homelands' for various ethnic groups). They champion ecological causes and campaign against chemical plants which threaten to pollute the atmosphere and further desecrate the motherland. Certainly, there is a strand of genuine nationalism in such feelings. So much has been pulled down, so much history has been perverted and distorted and suppressed, that it engenders a feeling of outrage and a determination to reclaim the past. People object to the fact that streets, towns, cities were named after criminals and thugs; they hate the fact that the pre-Revolutionary name of a stream or a neighbourhood has been forgotten even by the oldest inhabitants of the area.

However genuine feelings of nationalism may be, it came as a surprise to be told by a priest that anti-Semitism was no longer an issue in the Soviet Union and that the only religious antipathy was felt between Christians and Moslems. It took a while for me to realise he meant that Christians were no longer killing Jews but were instead being killed in Azerbaijan by Moslems. Nothing in his tone suggested that this was an improvement on the previous position.

Our Contemporary has about 200,000 subscribers, of whom about 30,000 live in Moscow, and advances a programme of what might be called strategic chauvinism. The editorial staff do not like to call themselves pure nationalists: nationalism is a taboo word. All nationalists in the Soviet Union are 'internationalists'. They admit to being Russian patriots and slavophiles but base their 'internationalism' on the claim that Russia, the sacred motherland, should retain its national identity in the same way as France or England or Holland. In a half-hearted attempt to tie their beliefs to Marxism they make great play of a pre-Revolutionary movement they call the agricultural commune, or brigade, or association of likeminded people who come together in the countryside to support one another. They see this idea as purely Russian and one which anticipates Marx. It is all nonsense of course, they are nationalists in the way that Le Pen in France or Eugene Terre'Blanche in South Africa are nationalists, and they are connected with, though careful to distance themselves from, such vociferous groups as *Pamyat*. Narrow-minded, intemperate, noisy, yet effective, these Russian nationalist groupings come as little surprise – indeed, in an African abroad they evoke feelings of powerful nostalgia. Tribal demagogues, anti-Semites, anticapitalist rhetoricians with earthy socialist leanings, who justify all the old diseases in the name of the 'modern' cure and always talk the same language: purity of blood, foreign infection, racial cleanliness, sacred soil, beloved motherland; angry tears, big biceps, black berets, boots.

The Russian Right delights in pointing out how many leading communists were Jewish: Trotsky, Bukharin, Kaganovich and others. There is a tendency which believes that the Revolution was the plot of certain Jewish intellectuals or, as they are referred to on the banners of the *Pamyat* organisation at their political meetings, 'the rootless cosmopolitans', a term resurrected from the Nazi past. These zealots march under the banners of Russian patriotism and demand, for instance, the restoration of the great Church of Christ the Saviour and other Russian monuments. Disguised as the authentic claims of civic-minded patriots, this is a code, a kind of fighting talk founded, for such is its angry lack of originality, upon hatred of Jews.

But the bruised little groups of real nationalists receive short shrift. A group of Crimean Tartars, survivors and descendants of those who were forcibly removed from the Crimea by Stalin, held a demonstration on the steps of the Lenin Library. They displayed a rather neatly worded banner: 'We demand the right to return to the Crimea.' The police rounded them up, confiscated their banners and took them away in buses. The whole demonstration couldn't have lasted more than ten minutes.

Around the apartment blocks the birch trees stand solitary, anorexic, albino. The crows are noisy. The returning commuters trudge along the snowy paths to their anonymous apartment blocks, bags in hand, heads down. In the twenties the Bolsheviks were convinced that the majority of the population were hostile to them. Stalin and Trotsky both believed that since the population were out to injure them the people should be beaten into obedience. Today attitudes to the ruling party have changed and the leaders are reaching out – only to find the bulk of the people utterly indifferent. Perestroika, political reform, means it is now legal to ask for more. But the effect is to reveal how little there is to give.

*

Most people prefer soap opera to politics. For some weeks a Brazilian soap opera called *Escrava Esaura* became an obsession in the city. The phone lines clogged after each daily episode as fans discussed the finer points. When the final episode was screened, across the city fans gathered in shops, offices, hotels, wherever there was a television set, and everything simply came to a halt. The climax was particularly exciting. The young heroine, who was being forcibly married to an idiot hunchback, was saved in the nick of time when the villain, who had suspiciously ginger hair and, we all knew, was up to no good, was dramatically unmasked. But the drama was not over for it looked as if the happy lovers would both be poisoned by a jealous enemy. At the last moment, the fatal cordial containing the poison was switched and in a moment of fine poetic justice the poisoner herself drained the lethal glass. All over Moscow housewives, floor ladies and shop girls, doormen, clerks, waiters, policemen and the girls at the Intourist desks of all the hotels wiped tears from their eyes as they watched the lovers united in marriage, while the slaves danced on the green fields of Brazil and threw their hats in the air. Then with a creak and a groan and a sigh all of Moscow got back to work.

'It was the clothes,' said Alya in her tunnel beneath the road. 'And the sun!'

'No, no, it was the capacity for realising their full economic potential,' said Victor the waiter.

Valentin, as ever, was closer to the mark.

'It was full of pretty things. Even the slaves had pretty things.'

If Hamlet were reading anything in Moscow today, it would probably be the shopping catalogue called *Vestnik*, a hundred and fifty pages long, five roubles a copy, full of shoes, cosmetics, radios, calculated to inflame the desires of Soviet consumers. The trouble is that the pretty dresses and the stereo systems so delightfully pictured are not available. Some were but are no longer. Some will be but are not yet. So at five roubles a throw you are getting a book full of pictures and 'words, words, words'. Valentin gazed at it mournfully. For twenty kopeks, he could go along to the Exhibition of Economic Achievements and see the same unavailable goods at a far cheaper price.

He had kept his *samizdat*, cherished editions of once forbidden authors, Nabokov, Pasternak, Akhmatova. Most of his collection was photostated from Russian editions published in the United States and rather beautifully bound in green and brown leather so that what was once an illegal object now had a look of beauty to it, the rather faded beauty of a relic. His remark about *samizdat* surprised me. It had probably been a mistake to collect it, he said, because the effect had been self-destructive.

'By reading the forbidden literature, by feeling ourselves to be different, we drifted apart from most people and we were lost.'

'Maybe before you leave us this time, you should get used to it by leaving Moscow on a rehearsal,' Valentin suggested with Byzantine logic, suspecting, quite rightly, that I would not be returning for some time.

So I went to a closed town in the Moscow region. They said it had been opened recently. I was the first foreigner to visit the place since the Revolution. No one knew why it had been closed and no one knew why it had been opened, no one knew anything and they did not know it in that delicate, rueful way that goes back longer than anyone cares to remember. We acted on the rumour that the place was now 'open' and proceeded from there, proceeded by car from Moscow, driven by one Vassily who had his mind on motor racing and ice hockey. In sporting matters he was a rough contact man. The clashes on the ice moved him to a kind of raw pleasure. And with motor racing it was not speed he doted on but the crashes. He deplored their scarcity, in most races, and he sighed long and often, a windy exhalation of boredom, resignation and regret for wasted ambitions, extinguished dreams. Vassily told me he planned to change his life but then 'something happened', and his plans always failed. He read his sports paper, slept longer and longer hours, drove, or rather aimed, his car down the long arrowed roads out of Moscow with weary precision, locked in his own impenetrable silence, a kind of terminal lassitude which made his shoulders sag beneath the weight of his boulder head, as if they were a wooden plank bending beneath a pumpkin left there too long; the way I remember Africans would weigh down the corrugated iron roofs of their huts. Let those who talk of glasnost and perestroika consider Vassily. The only time I ever saw him animated was when I asked him what he thought about the new reforms. He dropped his paper and banged himself on the forehead with his fist, like a man knocking at a door, but so hard I thought he would injure himself; then, receiving no reply, he stopped and went back to his paper. I never asked again.

Beside Vassily sat the man who had invited me to visit his closed town. He was a teacher of English at the local teachers' training college. 'A third-rate institute,' he explained cheerfully, 'but I like it there.'

This expression of happiness disturbed Valentin, who had come along for the ride. Fate had just dealt him a very Russian card. He had been invited to make an extended visit to the German Democratic Republic. As if recognising his quivering desire to voyage into the outer space of 'the world', he had been offered the dubious pleasure of a short visit to one of Mother Russia's nearby satellites. He had decided to reject the offer. 'If I go anywhere it only counts if it's somewhere I want to go.'

'And where do you want to go?'

'Barbados.'

'Well, maybe East Germany is a start.'

'Barbados or nowhere.'

The roads down which we sped were straight and seemed to go on for ever. They carried a slow solid stream of heavy traffic, lorries and trucks loaded with wood and textiles, bricks and cement. Private cars were few and far between. Moscow slipped behind and there was the holiday of seeing the little wooden houses with their painted eyes, a solitary pear tree, a vegetable patch. When they vanished the only sign of human habitation was the police post, little bunkers by the roadside where the policeman waits and watches as you pass – and when you think about it, there are so few private cars passing that the policeman has time to stare meaningfully as each goes by and the drivers look straight ahead; this was a mobile identity parade. The

Russians have the habit of mounting automobile wrecks on roadside platforms, much as the English dangled hanged men from gibbets to deter the populace. Curiously, it is always private cars that go on display though the bulk of the traffic is official, heavy trucks and lorries which must cause as many accidents, but then they are official, owned by the State, their drivers employees and their accidents private, secret, safeguarded. There is no one to blame. The lesson to be drawn from the display of these private steel skeletons is that individuals cause trouble.

The town that was closed was the creation of one man, a textile millionaire who virtually owned it in the early years of this century. Since the Revolution several more factories have been built, apartment blocks, and the Party headquarters, bulky, proud, vulgar. The millionaire's original factory remains and is still in use, rather beautiful in its crumbling red brick, and most imposing, stretching as far as you can see through the heart of the town. The English teacher told me that the millionaire had been a supporter of the Revolution. He had believed in it and had given all his money to the Bolshevik cause. A few minutes later he rephrased this. 'Actually, all his property was confiscated, but because he had strengthened the Revolution, he was later compensated for the money he had lost.' I chewed on this. The teacher came back again. 'Well, strictly speaking, the millionaire committed suicide soon after the Revolution. But his heirs were compensated for his losses. They had by then migrated to England.'

The millionaire had been an enlightened employer, even building an old-age home for his workers. The old-age home was now the teachers' college and little had been done to improve the building since it had been erected. I was shown where I might hand my coat and hat.

'Please undress in there,' said the English teacher encouragingly, 'then I will show you the toilet. There we will relieve ourselves.'

Relieved, I was led into a lecture hall. As I had discovered among the schoolchildren in Moscow, the young are alert, friendly, satirical, sceptical and warmhearted. If hope for the future lies anywhere it lies with the young people of the Soviet

Union. They demanded information on everything from American elections to the spread of Aids. They crowded the room, spilling out into the corridors, and those who spoke no English simply came to have a look at the first foreigner to come to town since the Revolution.

'What kept you?' asked a girl with red hair and astounding china-blue eyes.

The English teacher told me of 'the changes' taking place. 'We are all going to vote for the very first time. We are putting our rector up for election. Well, it is half an election because there is no other candidate. But he's a good fellow so I will certainly vote for him. I suppose it's not really an election, is it?'

'More of a vote of confidence.'

'Exactly!' He beamed. 'And we all have confidence in him.'

I ate lunch with the students. Chicken the colour of snow and almost as cold.

'Killing such birds seems a crime,' I remarked to the redhead.

'Killing it was a mercy,' she replied gently, 'eating it is the crime.'

When I left, after 'putting on my clothes' in the cloakroom and declining further offers to relieve myself, I noticed big black cars parked beside Vassily's battered Moskvitch, outside the rector's office. The editor of the student newspaper, an intense boy from the Ukraine, explained that the local Party big-shots were meeting in the college to discuss the bombardment of directives from Moscow ordering restructuring and democracy. Vassily dozed fitfully behind the wheel, his sports paper over his face, dreaming no doubt of icy collisions and blood-flecked car smashes. The black Party limousines grumbled softly in the falling snow, the drivers keeping warm.

'Do you think changes are coming?' I asked the young editor.

He shrugged. 'How can you make democratic changes when you have only one party?'

I said to Valentin, 'Perhaps you could visit some Eastern European country, like Hungary.'

'I prefer Paris.'

'Budapest *is* rather like Paris.'

'I have always disliked anything that looks *like* Paris, or tastes *like* caviar, or smells *like* a rose!'

Leaving Moscow is hateful, chiefly because you leave so many Muscovites behind. The knowledge that they are locked into the country torments and tantalises the dreamers. They dream of Barbados and Belgium and California, but they get, at best, a couple of weeks on the Black Sea. Departing foreign visitors disturb; they assume, in the eyes of those who insist on seeing them off, the bulky, space-suited, extra-terrestrial quality of intrepid space travellers.

When I left the last time, Felix, a film-maker, looked out at the drifting snow and advised, 'Best to come to Moscow in the spring, or summer.' Then in a low voice, thinking I could not hear him, or believing I would not understand him, he added to himself in Russian, 'Or best not to come at all . . .'

Felix made films for children. 'I'm so famous that if I get caught speeding, I mention my name and the militia man sends me on my way! They all know me.'

Special privileges accrue to special guests. When such arrangements favour some over others – well, that's life. When privileged arrangements go wrong – well then, as they say in Moscow, 'that's perestroika!'

The customs officer refused to allow me through the special barrier for privileged foreigners. He scrutinised my written permission to clear customs without the usual formalities, that is to say without the usual wait, and then perestroika intervened and I waited like everyone else. But I waited at the head of the queue. A very drunk Dutchman turned on me shouting that this was the most democratic country in the world, no class distinctions operated; it was a disgrace that I should pass to the head of the queue ahead of people who had been waiting patiently. I sympathised, of course, I understood his point. I had the impression he was not catching a plane himself – he just came out to the airport to fume at foreigners getting special treatment. He felt about foreigners the way the aspirant defector in the Georgian restaurant felt about blacks. Perhaps the Dutchman had been in Moscow too long. He had become knowledgeable. I suggested to him that he take his protest to the top. Perhaps he should picket the airport? Or complain to the minister? Or convey his feeling of outrage directly to the Central Committee? The Dutchman made a brief speech on equality. The Russian travellers were embarrassed. The customs officials were unmoved. My friends who had come to say goodbye were sunk in the depths of melancholy amusement.

Valentin came to the airport, whenever I left, and Nadia the philosopher, Viktoria, Vassily, and Victor the waiter turned arbitrageur, and Felix the film-maker. In a sense everybody came: the Hungarian chickens, the floor lady who kissed me and the missing muezzin, and Alya the streetwalker, and all my friends. And even if they did not really come – or had left the country themselves in dream or imagination years before, I had the sense of being accompanied to the point of departure by all these who bound me to Moscow. And, of course, my companions always wanted to know what was on 'the other side', when I had passed the barrier, when I had crossed over?

And what could I say? How could I tell them that nothing much happened? That the departure area was dull, until you were startled by the duty-free shop, a dizzying glimpse into the kingdom of Hermès and Aquascutum, like a rush of blood to the head; that the Irish assistants wore unexpected red tunics, as a mark of respect perhaps to the joint owners of the duty-free shop; that the *beriozka* shop was closed; the restaurant out of coffee; the eyes of the departing passengers glazed with relief. That I had once heard an American tell a friend that 'you go mad in Moscow for the pleasure of recovering your sanity when you leave'. That the aircraft sat heavily on the tarmac looking as if it was unlikely ever to get off the ground; that a man with a broom invariably stood at the top of the steps; a girl in dungarees was dropping blue plastic bags from the exit hatch; men in mackintoshes ran up and down the steps for no reason, perhaps taking exercise; that a muddy yellow Volvo would be drawn up beneath the aircraft wing, and that we all expected departure to be delayed.

I could say nothing of this because they would not believe me, and if I had been them I would not have believed me either. Instead, once I had passed through passport control I would raise two fingers in a victory sign, I would live up to expectation, I would wave like a cosmonaut.

Waiting to clear customs I looked up at the departure board and read off the destinations of departing flights, muttering to myself in a voice I thought no one else heard, 'Tokyo, Paris, London . . .' Then, in a whisper so low I thought it came from inside my head, Valentin continued the litany I had unreasonably, unhelpfully, complacently ended. 'Mars,' he whispered, 'Venus, Jupiter, Alpha Centauri . . .'

Also available in Minerva

Christopher Hope

LEARNING TO FLY

This astonishingly subversive collection of tales about South Africa by the author of *A Separate Development* and *My Chocolate Redeemer* is based on his award-winning collection *Private Parts* but contain a large element of new material. We meet Colonel Rocco 'Window Jumpin'' du Preez and Colonel Jake 'Dancin'' Mphalele, both top-flight security interrogators. Then there is Hilton, the student radical who out-radicalises them all including, eventually, himself in a surprising resurrection; and, most movingly, Ndbele, who has to create his own world in order to abide by the rules of a racially obsessed society.

Christopher Hope's vivid, humorous vision of both sides of South African life wickedly lays bare the absurdities of apartheid in a series of stories which is at once wry, savage, ironic and elegant.

'Not until the end of *Private Parts* can one fully appreciate the care, the skill, with which these ten short stories were assembled . . . The affect is insidious and devastating – a total flaying of the rationale with which apartheid is veiled. Beneath it, there is exposed so monstrous a travesty of reason that anyone (of whatever colour) attempting to live by its rules must themselves become mad in order to feel themselves sane . . . Other South African writers have said this, but none with such ferocious humour, creative imagination or style'
New Statesman

Christopher Hope

MY CHOCOLATE REDEEMER

'Bella is a teenage chocolate addict who listens to heavy metal music on her Walkman and is given to fits of praying and prying . . . Bella lives in a gossipy village by an idyllic lake in France with her aristocratic grandmother who adores the charismatic leader of a fascist political party dedicated to ridding France of its black citizens; and her uncle, a mad scientist who is attempting to duplicate the birth of the universe in his laboratory.

'This rather perverse, eccentric society is shaken by the appearance of a deposed African leader, an urbane man with a reputation for intense cruelty and cannibalism. Perhaps his unusual diet is what makes him so delectable, for he is Bella's chocolate daddy, his skin so dark and lustrous that she imagines eating him . . .

'A fantasy with realistic trappings . . . beautifully written with angry irony surging through the narrative' *Listener*

'A clever, wry and beautifully written novel about self-deception and the origins of despotism'
Guardian

'Unholy, stylish and very funny'   Elaine Feinstein,
Times

'Curious, alarming and exceptionally original'
Hermione Lee, *Irish Times*

Christopher Hope

A SEPARATE DEVELOPMENT

Winner of the David Higham Prize for the Best First Novel.

'*A Separate Development* is one of the best books ever written about South Africa'   Peter Porter, *Observer*

'Harry Moto, the adolescent hero of Christopher Hope's fine and very funny first novel, has problems with fallen arches, crinkly hair that won't flatten down, plump breasts and, for a white, unusually dark skin. Harry feels most inconvenienced by his over-developed breasts, which draw mercilessly sarcastic observation from his school mates, but as Harry lives in South Africa it is not surprising that it's his skin colour which eventually brings about his downfall . . .

'There is nothing intrinsically funny about Harry's fate nor the nature of the society in which he finds himself living, but Hope's comic vision of this crazy and tragic state of affairs expertly brings off the difficult feat of providing both an entertaining novel, rich in lovingly evoked detail and character, and a profound political indictment'   William Boyd, *Sunday Times*

'A remarkable first novel . . . exquisitely funny' *Literary Review*

Gita Mehta

KARMA COLA

'A book of stylish originality that simultaneously and outrageously so takes the mick out of the West and East that in her next avatar Gita Mehta will surely be the wit of the decade ... *Karma Cola* is almost uniquely funny and, like most funny things, essentially sad'   James Cameron, *Sunday Telegraph*.

'The scintillating flurry of anecdotes through which Gita Mehta describes the fools, knaves, wretches and occasional genuine sage she finds on the modern spiritual path is no less formidable than the old one-two of the Zen masters. *Karma Cola* is a highly entertaining account of the consumerist West struggling to gobble up Hinduism and choking itself in the process'   *The Listener*

'Her ear for accents and dialogue is wicked. The voices in the book are brilliantly done ... Ms Mehta shows that she can bring a scene alive with just a few brisk strokes and a dab of colour'   Jonathan Raban, *Sunday Times*

'It's as if Tom Wolfe had gone to India, changed his white suit for a dirty dhoti, and freaked out by the sacred ghats ... There are enough crazy characters, stories and wild scenes here for several novels, and the entire book offers what must be the real juice and colour of modern India seen from the inside' *Library Journal*

Paul Rambali

FRENCH BLUES

Traversing memory, encounter and anecdote, *French Blues* is a foray through the supermetro tunnels and graffiti-tagged suburbs of a France that can no longer recognise itself; where the *nouvelle* literature is the comic book and the most popular setting for romance a computer network.

Paul Rambali dines with *couture* king Christian Lacroix, dives into a limo with sex symbol Beatrice Dalle, explores Paris with veteran photographer Robert Doisneau, discusses Hyper-reality with Jean Baudrillard and attends a rally with 10,000 *Front National* supporters.

Revisiting the France of his childhood, the author discovers a quite unfamiliar country. Exotic, iconoclastic and enlightening, his unsentimental journey lays to rest outdated myths and recounts the stuff of new ones.

'A jazzy, sceptical portrait of modern urban France . . . Like a series of video-clips, naively provocative and steeped in a flashy, youthful cynicism, yet it does contain insights . . . He asks many of the right questions and arguably comes closer to the real France than many a romantic, rural Francophile' *Sunday Times*

'The first book for a long time to evoke a truly recognisable France. Rambali is a fine contemporary *flaneur*' *City Limits*

Peter Conrad

DOWN HOME

Tasmania is a strange place to be born – the offshore island of an offshore continent, regularly omitted from maps of Australia; a sad, lonely, savagely beautiful place which, in trying to forget its past of penal brutality and aboriginal genocide, has convinced itself that it's a demure little England, an Isle of Wight adrift twelve thousand miles from London. Peter Conrad grew up there, left in 1968, and after almost two decades went back to see the home he had lost, with its wild rivers, impassable rain forest, marsupial monsters and historical scars. In the process he discovered a small world he had never known: a Lilliput of wonders and oddities – his own home and the secret, forgotten birthplace of Australia. The result is an extraordinary book combining travel, autobiography and history, by a supremely versatile and penetrating critic of contemporary culture.

'A rich achievement'   Colin Thubron, *Independent*

'Erudite, imaginative, wide ranging'   *New Statesman & Society*

'Here is a work of real distinction, marked by Conrad's aboriginal cunning, which he nearly junked forever in leaving home'   *Sunday Times*

'A personal and literary triumph'   *Literary Review*

Brian Hall

STEALING FROM A DEEP PLACE

Equipped only with a small travel fellowship and a good map, Brian Hall rode his bicycle from England to Italy, where a chance conversation inspired him to extend his journey to the other side of the Iron Curtain.

As autumn gave way to winter, Hall rode hundreds of miles over mountainous roads in Romania and Bulgaria, sleeping in fields and abandoned haylofts to avoid paying the 'official' hotel prices. His unflagging enthusiasm sustained him through food shortages, petty bureaucracy and a truly spectacular equipment failure. His reward was the kindness of strangers, who opened their doors, and sometimes their hearts, to an insatiably curious visitor.

Stealing from a Deep Place will surely be hailed as a classic of travel writing, with its sharply etched portraits of rural citizens and their daily life. Sympathetic, wry and evocative, this is an extraordinary and stylish glimpse of a hidden world.

'A complex and often fascinating portrait of countries near to us but generally neglected' *Sunday Times*

'A refreshing book written with verve' *Country Life*

A Selected List of Titles Available from Minerva

The prices shown below were correct at the time of going to press.

Fiction

☐	7493 9026 3	**I Pass Like Night**	Jonathan Ames	£3.99 BX
☐	7493 9006 9	**The Tidewater Tales**	John Bath	£4.99 BX
☐	7493 9004 2	**A Casual Brutality**	Neil Blessondath	£4.50 BX
☐	7493 9028 2	**Interior**	Justin Cartwright	£3.99 BC
☐	7493 9002 6	**No Telephone to Heaven**	Michelle Cliff	£3.99 BX
☐	7493 9028 X	**Not Not While the Giro**	James Kelman	£4.50 BX
☐	7493 9011 5	**Parable of the Blind**	Gert Hofmann	£3.99 BC
☐	7493 9010 7	**The Inventor**	Jakov Lind	£3.99 BC
☐	7493 9003 4	**Fall of the Imam**	Nawal El Saadewi	£3.99 BC

Non-Fiction

☐	7493 9012 3	**Days in the Life**	Jonathon Green	£4.99 BC
☐	7493 9019 0	**In Search of J D Salinger**	Ian Hamilton	£4.99 BX
☐	7493 9023 9	**Stealing from a Deep Place**	Brian Hall	£3.99 BX
☐	7493 9005 0	**The Orton Diaries**	John Lahr	£5.99 BC
☐	7493 9014 X	**Nora**	Brenda Maddox	£6.99 BC

All these books are available at your bookshop or newsagent, or can be ordered direct from the publisher. Just tick the titles you want and fill in the form below. Available in:
BX: British Commonwealth excluding Canada
BC: British Commonwealth including Canada

Mandarin Paperbacks, Cash Sales Department, PO Box 11, Falmouth, Cornwall TR10 9EN.

Please send cheque or postal order, no currency, for purchase price quoted and allow the following for postage and packing:

UK	80p for the first book, 20p for each additional book ordered to a maximum charge of £2.00.
BFPO	80p for the first book, 20p for each additional book.
Overseas including Eire	£1.50 for the first book, £1.00 for the second and 30p for each additional book thereafter.

NAME (Block letters) ....

ADDRESS ....

....

....